*Errata*

THE NEW FACE OF COMMUNICATION

Through an inadvertence in paging, the exhibits on pages 107 and 121 have been transposed. What is shown on page 107 as "The Technical Model" is in fact the servo-system and should appear on page 121. What appears on page 121 as "The Servo-System" is in fact the technical model and should appear on page 107.

AMERICAN MANAGEMENT ASSOCIATION

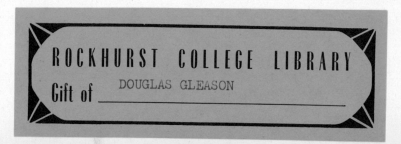

*The New Face*
*of Communication*

*Glenn A. Bassett*

# *The New Face*
# *of Communication*

American Management Association, Inc.

*To*
*Glenna Lynn*

# *Foreword*

—◆•⇐—

HOW DO YOU BEGIN A BOOK on communication? Do you bare your soul in order to establish some kind of personal relationship with the reader? Probably not; that is hard enough to do on a face-to-face, personal basis. Nor is it likely to have the ring of authenticity.

Do you look for some irresistible witticism or gimmick to capture the reader's attention? Certainly any good speechmaker would recommend such a course of action, but it doesn't seem appropriate to begin a discussion of communication on a note of strained relevance or superficiality.

Such alternatives reflect a real dilemma which every would-be communicator must face sooner or later: the question of purpose. Is it your purpose to supply information and perspectives which may help your audience develop an understanding of the subject, or is it your purpose to impress the reader and influence him to follow some predetermined course? If you select the first alternative, you presume to teach—a chancy activity at best, with few clear-cut payoffs or firm satisfactions. If you choose the second purpose, you presume to direct the lives of others—certainly an egotistical course of action, but one which serves the needs of business well and which can provide immediate gratification.

The central issue of Chapter 5 might be summarized as a question of choosing between communicating and performing. In this context, communicating is the act of being yourself—of expressing your personal views and sentiments without defensiveness or fear of controversy. It is informality, spontaneity, and openness for the purpose of sharing experiences and facilitating learning. Performance, on the other hand, involves acting out a prescribed part, in which the personality of the actor is subordinated to the role he plays and in which the object is to influence, impress, or entertain.

Here is a tenuous but useful distinction, because it points up the opportunity for the writer to play the expert and try to supply precast solutions or to opt for the role of a guide who merely presents new facts and fresh ideas. When, as an author, you consider the options with a clear head, it becomes obvious that whatever you try, you have set yourself an oversize task. And, when it is finished, you discover that it was impossible to limit yourself to one option and that you have followed one purpose, then the other.

In this instance, the primary purpose is to guide the reader over some fresh terrain which will expand his understanding of communication and, thereby, his ability as an effective communicator. Inevitably, there are also some formulas and recipes for communicating.

This book on communication thus begins by letting the reader know what the author's basic style is. In doing so it recognizes that, in order to communicate at all, you must respect the context you find yourself in as well as the expectations of your audience. You must begin from a fresh but conventional starting point. This is a tall order, and, as with the writing of the book itself, you can only put your best efforts to it and be prepared to live with the result. But that is what you have to do whenever you want to communicate.

Let's get on with it.

# *Acknowledgments*

————◆————

WRITING A BOOK during your evening and weekend hours has some drawbacks, but it is a rewarding experience in at least two respects: First, the discipline of putting your ideas into some semblance of order and investigating them for their viability and potential is an intensely stimulating and satisfying activity in its own right. Second, since it is impossible to do the whole job alone, given the limitations of time and energy, you must seek help wherever you can find it. The selflessness and even eagerness with which that help is forthcoming are themselves enough to justify the effort.

I am indebted to several people for the important contributions they made to the reality of this book. The first acknowledgment must be to my wife, whose efforts as critic, morale booster, and typist of each manuscript draft were indispensable. Hers is the support that only a devoted wife could provide. In addition, there are those among my colleagues in the General Electric Company who gave freely of their time and support. Dwight Meader, a man of great courage and dedication to the improvement of interpersonal communication, Harvard Weatherbee, a manager who values truth above authority, and Roger Hawk, who taught me what supportive and effective managerial communication is really all about, each contributed invaluable suggestions to the improvement of the manuscript. Finally, it is only

7

appropriate to acknowledge the skilled efforts of my AMA editors, whose contribution to the readability and good sense of this volume is a major one. Certainly, without the aid of these people, the job could not have been done. Their combined efforts can only leave one with a sense of gratitude and humility.

—G. A. B.

# Contents

# PART ONE

*The Elements*

*of Communication*

# 1

---•◆•---

# *What Is Communication?*

"IT ALL BOILS DOWN to communication." This was a familiar line, and Harvey Hancock had used it at least three times in the past hour. Now, however, he said it with added emphasis. His tone was the kind he normally used when he gave instructions to a subordinate. It was deliberate, even a little pompous, and the line was delivered with jaw slightly set, which gave the appearance of determination and seriousness. "That's our trouble; we don't communicate." This time Harvey got a rise out of his fellow conference members. From one corner of the room came the retort, "I wish you'd tell me what you mean by communication," followed by another jibe from the opposite corner. "Yeah, you're sure not communicating with me."

Harvey was visibly shaken by the sharpness of the responses to his attempt to be helpful. He had come to this seminar fully expecting to get some fresh ideas on how to communicate with people, and up to this point he had been quite disappointed. He had heard little that was really new in the discussions on the techniques of conference leadership or in the lectures on how to appraise performance. He frequently found himself thinking, "I already do that regularly!" Harvey was beginning to feel he was something of an expert in this field, and his intent in reaffirming his faith in communication was to show that his heart was in the right place. So why the strong reaction? Why couldn't they accept the fact that he was merely trying to help?

A voice came from the front of the room: "We've done a lot of talking about communicating here, but as far as I can see we're doing a lousy job of communicating with one another on the subject." Harvey winced. He looked toward the seminar leader in hope of finding some support. But the leader's eyes were focused on a light fixture about eight feet to Harvey's right, and his mouth was set in a thin, mocking smile. Harvey could think of nothing to do but point out the error of his colleagues' ways.

"Now, look, fellows. We all know what communication is. Don't we? Of course we do!" Harvey was good at answering his own questions. He did it regularly. "You want to inform your employees about a change in holidays, so you check it out with your personnel people and your legal consultants; then, if everything is O.K., you go to your communications man. You tell him to write up something that will let the employees know you've changed the holidays and you're sure they'll all be in agreement with the change. Or you want to let a guy know where he stands on the job, so you bring him in, sit him down, and tell him what a good job he's doing; then you level with him on his problems. You communicate with him face to face and let him know exactly what you want." Harvey emphasized his words and was careful of his enunciation to make sure that no one misunderstood him.

The irreverent voice from the other side of the room piped up again. "When was the last time your manager did that to you?"

"My manager and I have an excellent working relationship. We talk over our problems every day of the week, just like clockwork, and we never have any difficulty understanding what is needed."

The irreverent one persisted. "Yeah, Harv. But when was the last time your manager called you in, buttered you up, and then gave it to you in the gut about all your faults?"

Harvey's reaction was immediate and instinctively defensive. "That's not how I appraise people! The way you say it makes it sound like bringing cattle in for slaughter."

There was a dull silence for a moment. Finally, the seminar leader spoke up. "I think Harvey is at least trying to be honest with us about this," he said. "But I'm afraid we've done a lot of talking about communication without ever really getting down to the nub of things. We haven't defined what communication really is."

"I can't believe there's anyone here who doesn't know what communication is," Harvey responded.

"We all have had experience in communicating," answered the instructor, "and I'm sure we have some sense of what communication is all about. I don't think, though, that we know in our brains what it really is. Perhaps we should stop wrangling and begin talking about communication the way a communications engineer would talk about it. Let's put aside our evangelical fervor while we examine some of the nuts and bolts of the process. Is that a satisfactory course to follow?"

General noises of assent arose from those in attendance. Harvey, however, was not among those agreeing. He felt betrayed, but he wasn't sure whether the seminar leader had betrayed him or whether he had betrayed himself.

## Nuts and Bolts: From Bits to Semantics

Without the medium of spoken language to transmit ideas and information from one person to the next, or from one generation to the next, we would certainly be living in a world very different from the one we know. Language permits each generation to stand upon the shoulders of the last and to reach for higher and higher goals. Each new generation is not doomed to start from scratch; rather, much that is wise and useful and helpful is available to each in the form of language. Our problem, perhaps, is that we take too much of this wisdom for granted because we have never had to ask for it or consider how we receive it or transmit it. The result is that we seldom get down to cases and only rarely define what we mean by communication.

An interesting illustration of nonverbal communication occurred recently during a discussion with the manager of a large clerical component in a major corporation. At one point this man's attention was suddenly diverted. His eyes turned toward the door and focused on the activity outside his office. He no longer heard his visitor; his thoughts were elsewhere. Faced with this intense attitude, the visitor could only stop talking and listen for whatever the manager seemed to be hearing, yet nothing extraordinary was audible. Then the manager turned back to his visitor, smiled, and said, "Whenever things get quiet out there, I know something is wrong. Sometimes it's only that lunchtime has caught up with me without my being aware of the hour. In the middle of the day, though, I know I'd better move fast and find out what's going on. The last time it happened, everybody was at the window watching a fire several blocks away. If you don't keep your eyes and ears open around here, everything occasionally grinds to a halt."

As he explained matters, it seemed so simple merely to listen for noise or the lack of noise as an indicator of the level of activity. But is this communication? Wasn't it a special kind of cue that alerted this particular manager to problems or distractions among his employees?

In point of fact, anything that conveys information is a kind of communication. In its simplest and least ambiguous form, communication is a light or buzzer signal that is either on or off. Consider, for example, the air-raid siren or the fire alarm. Each is an elementary kind of communication employed to advise people of hazards which may, if unattended, result in serious injury or death. Or, on a less dramatic level, consider the voltmeter and oil-pressure indicator in many modern automobiles. At one time nearly all automobiles were equipped with small dials to indicate the relative levels of voltage flow and oil pressure. Typically, both fluctuated somewhere around "normal" when the automobile was operating. The movement of the needle, however, was so gradual that a failure in the oil pressure or the electrical system could occur without warning.

To be sure, the information was there in complete form. Anyone willing to take the time to look at the gauges could determine whether the oil pressure or voltage was adequate. But changes in the reading were so subtle as to be missed all too frequently. In the end, car manufacturers changed to a simple on/off system of lights which conveys only the basic information—the system is O.K. or it is not—in such a way as to alert the driver to either a sudden or a gradual change. Some drivers regretted the loss of the information provided by the old gauges and needles. But the typical driver is undoubtedly just as happy to have in his car a system of communication that is less ambiguous, much more readily attended to, and reliably understood.

Communication in its most basic form is, indeed, an on/off, yes/no, present/absent process. The presence of a characteristic odor tells us that our dog has had an encounter with a skunk. The presence of footprints in freshly laid concrete tells us that someone has ignored the "keep off" sign. The presence of fossils in a particular rock stratum tells the geologist what forms of life existed at some period in the earth's history. An accumulation of newspapers on the front lawn tells others that we are not at home.

Communications engineers call the amount of information that a message possesses a "bit." A bit, however, is not necessarily a very small quantity. It may be a very small *or* a very large quantity since it is the amount of information needed to reduce the available alternative choices by exactly 50 percent by dividing all meaningful choices into two mutually exclusive ("yes" or "no") categories.

Everything from very simple to very complex options may be covered by bits. According to the story, one or two lights were to be hung in the tower of the old North Church in Boston to advise Paul Revere that the British were coming. The absence of light was to be the signal that the British were *not* coming; a single light, that they were coming by land; two lights, that the approach was by sea. Thus, by using lamps, two bits of information could be transmitted. The first bit was, "They are coming/they are not coming"; the second was, "They are coming by land/they are coming by sea." Technically, of course, the information transmitted by this process need not have been so limited. If knowledge of the approximate size of the troop movement had also been needed, a yellow lamp might have been used to indicate a small force, a red lamp to indicate a large force. In any event, Paul Revere and his compatriots were able to communicate the essential information reliably and effectively with their simple tools. They were probably unaware of the technical aspects of their communication, but this made them no less able to use the methods of transmission available at that time.

The radio and the telephone have made communication much easier and much more reliable, particularly for those of us who have difficulty remembering whether one lantern meant "by land" or "by sea." Modern techniques permit us to communicate in the manner that is most direct and meaningful to each of us as an individual. These techniques use much the same principles that Paul Revere and his friends used on the night of April 18, 1775—some kind of signal that can be varied to indicate predetermined meaning and intent. With radio, for instance, communication is effected by transmitting a steady signal which is "modulated" (that is, systematically altered or changed) to reflect differences between, say, voices and musical instruments. The signal is not on and off except to the extent that if a radio is off the air when it should be on, we may have a cue that something is wrong. Even in transmitting Morse code, the signal is subject to a wide range of variations that reflect differences in message elements; and voice transmission is far more complex. At its core, however, this type of communication consists of bits of information, and communicative elaborations are built on our capacity to transmit on/off, yes/no pieces of data from one person to another.

Many of our day-to-day communication problems stem from the fact that our tools of communication, including language, have progressed so far beyond the unambiguous simplicity of single bits of information that they are now only vaguely based on those bits. When we carry on a conversation, much of our language has something of the quality of a shorthand approach to communicating. We often use a word or phrase to convey information about kinds of behavior of which we approve or disapprove. Take the word "morality." An individual is "moral" if he obeys the law, refrains from stealing the property of others, is faithful to his wife and charitable to the poor, and so on. Or is he? Must other requirements be met to achieve morality? Are there instances in which one or more of the aforementioned requirements may *not* be met, yet the individual may be considered moral? Is it also necessary to refrain from drinking, smoking, dancing, and swearing in order to be moral? To a large segment of the population, morality is the avoidance of just these kinds of behavior; to other substantial segments, being involved in any or all of them is completely moral.

To cite another example: Is it moral to break a law which is in conflict with religious teachings? Some people would insist that failure to break the law is immoral under these circumstances.

Unfortunately, a great many of the concepts we commonly use in our day-to-day communication with one another are comparable to that of morality. Even some of our more common terms are loaded with potential ambiguity. "Automobile," for example, means "self-propelled," but we do not normally use the word to describe a motor scooter, which is self-propelled; nor do we use it for a farm vehicle that hauls a plow. Someone who is not familiar with the conventions of usage, but who has studied the roots of our language, might therefore be trapped into saying "automobile" to mean any one of several other types of vehicles. Were we to try to communicate with such a person, considerable confusion could arise. Indeed, the popular comedy program called "The Beverly Hillbillies" is built almost entirely on semantic misunderstandings; the simple hill folk mistake the complex concepts which are so glibly employed by the sophisticated city-slicker types who surround them. Programs such as this might lead us to conclude that there is little chance of effective communication between disparate cultures except to the extent that a member of one group is tolerant in his dealings with members of another.

Almost any sampling of plays—comedies and tragedies alike—will in fact reveal that an essential element of most plots is some sort of misunderstanding stemming from different interpretations of the same word or concept. To be sure, entertainment of this sort helps to point out potential misunderstandings in our culture and our language and may thereby reduce to some degree the occurrence of those misunderstandings. But the number of concepts that can be misunderstood seems endless. It is therefore likely that we can look forward to many comedies of the Beverly Hillbillies type and that misunderstanding will continue to occur in communication between people.

The point is that words are used by different people in different ways. We can overcome this problem to some extent by using substitute (or redundant) words in addition to, or in place of, any given concept. Nevertheless, when we try to communicate with another person we may have to go through a lengthy process of comparing our respective definitions of concepts. Inevitably, we find differences which must be resolved or identified so that we can be aware of the different ways in which each of us interprets each particular concept. Unfortunately, people seldom take the time in advance to decide on definitions for the central concepts of a conversation. More typically people blunder along much as Harvey's group did, only to find to their intense frustration that agreement and understanding are not easy to come by. Yet we can predict from experience that when two parties to a conversation use the same concepts to arrive at diametrically opposed conclusions, they will seldom stop and define what each concept means to each person. Instead, tempers rise and invectives are hurled. "You don't know what you're talking about" is a far more prevalent next step than is the candid admission, "Apparently we aren't talking about the same thing." Resorting to recriminations and anger in these circumstances is one sign that communication has broken down (indeed, cordiality usually indicates understanding, and coolness or anger signals breakdown in communication). It would be more effective, however, to admit that something has gone wrong and to evaluate the communication process.

The most usual problem, of course, is semantic confusion. In other words, the parties to the discussion use the same terms to mean different things, yet neither person informs the other of his definition of any given concept. Sometimes the solution is to avoid using highly abstract terms and to rely more heavily on terms for which the definitions are precise and unambiguous. Unfortunately, this is not always possible; certain terms—freedom, profit, responsibility, and the like—are too useful in our day-to-day communication. We should be on the lookout, however, for the inevitable difficulties. When someone says, "You're talking about something altogether different," it's time to begin examining the respective definitions of the concepts in question or to avoid semantic confusion by using alternate terms which have similar meanings. This helps make the concepts clearer and permits the listener to examine the message from more than one perspective.

## The Functions of Communication

Several years ago, a monthly periodical of note carried an article by a former reporter for a national news magazine. The substance of his argument was that the news weeklies claim to report only the facts to their reading publics, whereas, in reality, their columns are filled with heavily biased interpretations of the news. For a brief time, the argument flared; then the furor blew over. After a time, however, advertising began to appear for one of these news magazines suggesting that readers who wanted to be sure of getting "the facts" should read its columns. Clearly, such an advertising message implies that the publisher and his staff believe people value unbiased, factual reporting above reporting that is colored by the opinions of writer, editor, or advertiser.

They are probably right. A number of phrases in our language imply that people value facts much more highly than they do opinions. In the course of an argument, someone suggests, "Let's stick to the facts." The defense attorney in the courtroom says to the jury, "The prosecutor contends that my client is guilty of this crime. But let's look at the facts."

We are all too frequently assailed by the admonition that we ought to abandon opinions and look only at facts in attempting to solve problems. Unfortunately, suggestions to the effect that one person has a closer line on the facts than another or that one news magazine is more factual—that is, less biased—than another tend to be a bit hollow. The simple truth is that we interpret nearly all the events we perceive in the course of a lifetime, and our interpretations are heavily weighted with our biases and preferences.

For example, we see a man walk into an office building at nine o'clock in the morning. He is dressed in a gray flannel suit and is carrying a briefcase and a newspaper. He looks, in short, exactly like an executive arriving for work. If we were to stand at the same place and observe many more similarly dressed men pass us at the same hour, all carrying briefcases and newspapers, we would probably reach the same conclusion as to their roles and motivations. Were we to investigate further, however, we might discover that our conclusion was seriously in error, at least in a few cases. One of our "executives" might well be the building superintendent, who takes the elevator down to the basement, changes clothes, and attends to the furnace. Another might prove to be an ex-GI who works as a stock clerk during the day and spends his evenings studying engineering. So, even though our inferences about the men we have observed are correct by and large, in those cases where we are wrong we are likely to be *terribly* wrong.

Then there is the story of the American pilot who, during the Korean conflict, invariably showed up for a mission with a large briefcase stuffed full of maps and charts designed to aid him in getting to his assigned target and back. At any rate, this was the assumption that everyone made—until one day somebody new to the squadron said to the pilot, "You must carry an awful lot of maps and charts in your briefcase." The pilot responded, "Oh, no. These aren't charts. This is my lunch." He opened the briefcase to reveal a large thermos and an enormous supply of sandwiches. "Flying makes me hungry," he said.

The point is well taken; we need not strain to find comparable instances. Appearances can be, and often are, deceiving. We too frequently overlook the fact that most of the data we rely on in our day-to-day observations involve *assumptions and inferences rather than facts*. We see a man and a woman walking in the park with two small children. Immediately we infer that they are a family. Our inference is probably correct, but we may be wrong. Our "family" may be a brother and sister taking a walk with two of the neighbors' children or merely a group of people who look like a family. If we were to see a car plow into this group, we might report *as a fact* that we have seen a family—mother, father, and two children—killed in the park that morning. And, in so doing, we would believe implicitly and unquestioningly in the validity of the "facts" we were imparting.

Much of the information we use in conversation consists of interpretations of events that we have observed only in part and that appear to fall within a standard category we have developed out of our experiences. We normally accept appearances pretty much without questioning them. This is a reasonable and sensible strategy of perception, most of the time, because it permits us to deal efficiently with great masses of information. Over a given period, the odds are that most of our interpretations will be correct. However, by continually coloring the meaning of the events we witness, we limit ourselves to dealing almost entirely with inferences, biases, and opinions rather than with facts.

This limitation creates some problems in determining the purpose of any communication. Do we need to convey facts, or do we need to convey inferences? Or—to phrase this question from a new perspective—are we trying to inform, or are we trying to influence? These are the basic functions of communication: to inform and to influence.

## The Communicator's Two Options

In our everyday communication, we have two options: We can pass on raw, unprocessed facts; that is, we can describe the physical elements of the events we have observed—which might require us to say, for instance, that we saw a man dressed in a dark business suit and carrying a briefcase entering the building at nine o'clock this morning. Or we can convey information which we have processed, summarized, and added more meaning to—beyond the facts we have perceived. This is what we do when we say we saw an "executive" going to work at nine o'clock. Whichever approach we take, we may be convinced that we are merely informing someone of what happened rather than attempting to influence him in any way.

However, when we process information before passing it on, when we expand upon it and embellish it into conclusions that go beyond the hard facts, something happens to our communication: It begins to take on the flavor of our personality. The inferences and conclusions that we use in our "informative" conversations reflect our personal needs and interests to an increasing degree. And, in passing the information on, we expect it to be believed. We want people, in effect, to perceive the world exactly as we perceive it and to accept it, without question, exactly as we accept it.

As soon as we leave the realm of facts about the events we see, we begin to move into the realm of influence. No longer are we content to let those with whom we communicate interpret the facts for themselves and draw their own inferences. Having witnessed an event, we demand the privilege of establishing its meaning and importance. We insist on the accuracy of our own interpretation of it; we demand that anyone interested in knowing about the event accept our interpretation of it as accurate and unbiased.

It is only a short step to the patently persuasive communication. At this point, it may no longer be our intent simply to inform; rather, we set out to misinform in hopes of obtaining the "right" response from the people we are trying to influence. The door-to-door salesman who advises us that he is "not selling anything, but only placing copies of this magnificent new encyclopedia in selected homes in this neighborhood" is misinforming us in order to influence us. So is his fellow salesman who asks us, "Have you received your free gift from the Snazzy Cookware Company?" and, if we say no, declares, "I'll take care of that right away." In this age of the hard sell, the world is filled with smooth approaches and gimmicks designed specifically to influence a potential customer in the direction of buying. Communication in these cases is unabashedly used to influence consumer behavior.

And, whatever his efforts at persuasion and influence, the door-to-door salesman is an amateur compared to some parents and some managers. A mother says, "If you won't be a good boy, I'll have to call a policeman and get him to put you in jail," or, "Grandma doesn't bring toys to bad little girls." In a similar vein, a manager says to a job applicant, "The people who get ahead in this outfit are the ones who put the business ahead of themselves; they work long hours, and they're loyal through and through." Yet the fact may be that the only people who get ahead in the company are those who have a particular kind of degree or who marry into the family.

The extent to which people employ fantasy and fabrication to motivate others is amazing. Attempts to influence people through communication are, in fact, so common in our culture that they have produced a generation of skeptics. People have learned the principle of *caveat emptor* through hard experience with influencers out to sell not only products but also points of view. The proliferation of the salesman, not to mention the pitchman and the con man, during the past century has given most of us occasion to learn this lesson the hard way. People appear to be much less amenable now than they once were to the influence of fast talk. In the meantime, influence has taken on many new and fresh forms, and it is frequently impossible to know whether or not someone who is communicating with us is attempting to influence our actions.

One of the things we quickly learn about communication is that, no matter what the other person's intention, he probably is presenting his personal point of view, not giving us unprocessed facts. Typically, whether we find that point of view acceptable depends more on how it squares with our own experiences and convictions than on whether our informant seems to have enough facts to support it. All the communication with which we deal is loaded with human bias. Indeed, to get at the truth it is often necessary to begin by ascertaining exactly what that bias amounts to. This is the informal parallel to the suggestion made during the news magazine controversy that the best magazines to read are those that have a clear and unmistakable bias. The reader can then factor this known bias into his reading of the news and come out with his own approximation of the truth.

There is probably a good deal of sense in this suggestion. In a business environment, for example, it is almost always easier to deal with someone whose biases and convictions are known than with someone who successfully conceals his thinking. The person we are most likely to fear is the one we believe capable of subtly and cleverly influencing our behavior without our knowing it. The man who purports to be the processor of facts and who claims to be completely objective and free from bias in his use of facts to solve problems and arrive at decisions is, we suspect, the man who is most likely to be trying to influence those decisions along the lines of his own preferences. Human beings—to repeat—deal almost entirely in inferences, preferences, and personal points of view. They are sometimes more and sometimes less objective and unbiased, but they are almost totally unaccustomed to dealing with hard, cold, bare facts in working out their problems.

As we try to communicate, therefore, we do a little informing and a lot of attempted influencing. Many people, as we have noted, are even willing to misinform in order to influence the behavior of others. However, some progress toward recognition of our persistent use of inferences is possible and would be a step in the direction of communicating more informatively.

The matter of influencing people is another matter. It is one thing to try to influence people without their knowing that they are being influenced; it is something quite different to make your position and desires known and permit the other person to agree or disagree with your point of view.

One of the first problems that Harvey Hancock and his fellow conferees will have to face and understand in their efforts to communicate is this: In order to communicate effectively, we must be aware that most of our communications are aimed not at reaching an understanding with the other person but at directing and controlling him. Harvey's pronouncements, for example, were really intended to cow his listeners into accepting what he had to say and acknowledging his authority. The fact that he could not directly influence them should not be interpreted as a failure; instead, it should be recognized that this was the first time he had been given the opportunity to know the truth about this aspect of his communicating style. In a situation where Harvey was not the boss and could not use sanctions and punishments to bring people into line, he could no longer ride roughshod over them and insist that his understanding must also be their understanding. This minor conflict, however, is only the top of the iceberg. Indeed, Harvey may as well sit back and relax, because a tremendous amount of ground remains to be covered in this conference.

# 2

———————◄◆►———————

## *Influence and Control*

## *Through Communication*

FOR HUMAN BEINGS communication starts at birth. Much of the growing up is essentially a process of learning how to use words as a means
of dealing with the world.

In his adjustment to the people who surround him, many a child
learns first of all that the simplest way to gain notice is to scream. If
his parents' nerves are strong enough, and if they are sophisticated
enough to know that responding to his screams will only encourage
more of the same, they try to teach him that wailing does not guarantee immediate attention. They wait eagerly for the earliest signs of
their child's ability and willingness to talk, and they encourage a
"mama" or "dada" from him. Soothing sounds become rewards in
themselves to parent and child alike.

Thus parents make early use of language as a way of controlling
the child. But, as he develops further, becomes more active, and begins to creep and crawl, they are forced to use physical restraint as

well. And eventually they combine force with such symbolic methods as the loudly stated "No!" which nearly every mother uses with her newly mobile offspring. The child reaches toward the hot stove. Mother shouts, "No, no! Hot!" The child touches the hot surface and recoils. Two or three repetitions of this "No, no," coupled with a painful experience of some sort, condition the average child to draw back whenever "No, no!" is shouted at him.

For some parents, the training of children boils down to a simple formula: *Tell 'em and hit 'em.* They combine words with a stiff swat. When spoken commands are clear and unambiguous (that is, easy to discriminate from other verbal cues) and when the commands are consistently accompanied by what psychologists call "reinforcement" (either punishment or reward), the tell-'em-and-hit-'em approach can be very successful. It is a technique that has been used to train animals as well as children for centuries.

As the child matures, however, we become a little less primitive in our training techniques and begin to use a somewhat more sophisticated form of communication to control behavior. Perhaps we feel a little ashamed of ourselves for hitting the child, or perhaps it is sometimes difficult to apply physical force. We need a more convenient means of control, and so we begin experimenting with words as a means of controlling behavior at longer distances and over longer spans of time (that is, without immediate reinforcement).

## Building Long-Term Expectations

Typically, at this stage, parents resort to the promise of rewards that will be forthcoming at some point in the future: for example, "on Christmas morning" or "when we go to the store." And, to control the child more effectively when he is beyond our immediate reach, we use some such mythical figure as Santa Claus or the good fairy who knows and sees all his faults and virtues.

The child hitherto has been unaware that his parents are watching him or that he has been leaving obvious clues to his activities. Now he realizes that what he does is known—although, to the best of his knowledge, he has kept it secret. He may therefore decide that Santa Claus, good fairies, and his parents are indeed all-knowing and all-seeing.

Having established the thesis that there are agencies capable of knowing everything a child does and thinks, we then take the next easy step—to the assertion that everything he does that is "bad" or "naughty" will sooner or later be punished. Now we begin to define what we consider good and bad for the child. Virtue, we declare, is its own reward, but sin will surely be known and punished. We have arrived at that sophisticated level where we can control his behavior through fear of punishment and, even more efficiently, through a sense of personal guilt.

## Not a Self-Regulating Process

That this approach to the control of childhood behavior is effective goes without saying. Parents with large families could scarcely do without it. Training children to respond to verbal cues is one of the most important things we do in preparing them to live in a complex, civilized society. Unfortunately, however, the process is not self-regulating. It can be overdone or ignored altogether, and when we go to either extreme the results can be tragic.

If training in response to verbal cues is neglected or is badly butchered, a child may turn out to be "incorrigible." Or he may be so reckless and irresponsible that he must be held under immediate physical control virtually every minute; otherwise, he is likely to undertake some hazardous action that could be harmful to himself or to others.

Of course, a certain amount of systematic effort is necessary to train a child *not* to respond to verbal commands, although this often is misunderstood by parents. The trouble is that some parents are inconsistent; sometimes they reward and sometimes they punish the child for the same behavior—a pattern that is likely to confuse him rather than train him, at least in the early stages.

Yet other parents overdo training, and the use of punishment which is harsh or painful enough to break the spirit of the recalcitrant child may train him to overrespond to words. As a result, he may even become incapable of generating his own behavior—that is, making a decision for himself. He may become totally dependent on command inputs from external authority before he can take any kind of action.

## Faith in Words

What has all this to do with the adult world? Simply this: The training of children to respond to verbal commands is the basic process through which human beings learn to accept control by means of communication at school and on the job. It should come as no surprise that the communication techniques typically used by businessmen in memoranda, speeches, and employee newsletters are almost identical to the techniques used by parents to inculcate responsiveness to verbal commands.

A considerable amount of management is predicated, for example, directly on the tell-'em-and-hit-'em theory of communication. The first thing many new employees learn is a list of rules and the penalties which will be imposed for their infraction. "Smoking in the paint storeroom is cause for immediate discharge." "Unauthorized tardiness for three days in any month will result in a warning notice being prepared by the employee's supervisor and placed in the employee's file." "Employees apprehended in the theft of company property will be discharged and prosecuted." These are characteristic words used to describe prohibited behavior and the punishments to which they supposedly—but not invariably, as the new man soon learns—will lead.

On the job, employees may be bombarded with words of wisdom. "Profits equal jobs." "The safe worker is the smart worker." "Competitive conditions are critical in our industry at present. It is the responsibility of every employee to prevent waste, to put in a fair day's work for a fair day's pay, and to strive to keep our company competitive in this aggressive new market." Thus the businessman seems to have a boundless faith in the use of words to influence the behavior of his fellow man, particularly when that fellow man is an employee, even though little effort is made to follow up on those words or mete out the penalties decreed.

## Verbal Ability Equals Power

Nearly everyone, in fact, goes through a period of great confidence in the power of words to solve all his problems and concerns.

At about the turn of the century, the United States as a nation experienced one such period. At that time, almost any controversial issue was a ready subject for debating, which was a highly developed social activity and eventually became a form of simultaneous entertainment and instruction. Lectures were equally popular; an authoritative individual who could speak with enthusiasm and conviction was capable of moving people to all kinds of action. People appeared to believe that if only they could find the right words, they would command the solution to almost any problem.

We still cling to this faith in the magic of words. The youngster, particularly if he is bright, experiences a great deal of pleasure when he first learns how words can startle, mystify, and otherwise obtain responses from his parents and his peers. Unusually effective command of the language is the surest route to the highest levels of academic success; the verbally fluent youngster is almost inevitably the successful student.

The example thus set teaches its own lesson to each oncoming generation: Words are powerful medicine. The ability to use words well in writing or speaking is the ability to control many of the elements of one's environment—including parents, teachers, fellow students, and bosses. Observe the ease with which a voluble magician can convince youngsters, and even some oldsters, of the power of his abracadabra to change an egg into a rabbit or a handkerchief into a bouquet. In many respects, we are only a short way beyond the primitive tribe which still believes in black magic and the power of the witch doctor's curses!

Nor should we discount this power that words do obviously have. The employee who seems inept because he lacks skill in expressing himself may be classified as unpromotable by the manager and as a little stupid by his co-workers. As a general rule, such a person will accommodate his manager and friends by acting according to their perception of him, just as one who is seen as loyal and capable will do his best to live up to that reputation and another who is considered untrustworthy and lazy frequently loses his initiative or motivation to do a good job. It is almost as if he were trying to please by confirming the impression others have of him.

So much has been written about the power of positive thinking in dealing with problems that there is no need to belabor the subject here. However, the theory that "believing in something can make it come true" has been found correct so often that, despite its patent superficiality, it is not easily disregarded. Unquestionably, sufficient faith combined with effective effort can change the shape of the world and the course of human events. And, in exactly the same way, the words we use to describe people may, if we are persistent enough in using them, become true. Recent research on the impact of managerial evaluations of employees, as expressed indirectly through salary actions, has demonstrated that employees who are well thought of continue to improve in their performance, while those whose performance is described as poor tend, at best, to remain stable or, at worst, to lose ground.

## Words as Symbols

Certain it is that our ability to transmit a rich cultural heritage and our capacity for knowing one another and for solving complex human problems depend upon words. Having placed language on the altar of culture and bowed deeply before it, however, let us now strip away the overtones of black magic and cut this whole issue of verbal communication down to size.

Words are symbols. They stand for real things, real events, real feelings. They have no meaning in and of themselves unless we anchor them to the things, events, or feelings they are intended to represent. If we have no knowledge of Swahili and happen to hear two people talking in that language, the only power their words are likely to have over us is to make us feel excluded, confused, or just plain frustrated. If the most powerful Swahili incantations were to be uttered in our presence, we would not know what effect the words were intended to have. *The symbols we call words have power only to the extent that we know their meaning.*

The older sister who says to her infant brother, "I wish you weren't so stupid!" must initially give her words emphasis by using an angry tone. If her brother still cannot talk and the words are spoken pleasantly, he will understand only the tone, not the words, and will accept the statement as if it were a positive communication—that is, one of affection. If, however, the term "stupid" is used frequently in a strongly negative way, the small boy will begin to recognize it not only because of its sound but also because of the people it is applied to, and he will come to sense that "stupid" is something he doesn't want to be. He will recognize that it has overtones of incompetence and general worthlessness and is used to express dislike. Now, when his older sister says angrily, "You're stupid," he is devastated; he feels a sense of rejection that he may never have experienced before.

It is in this ability to convey rejection that the power of the word lies. In itself it is no more than a six-letter, two-syllable verbal symbol. For the small boy, however, it has acquired a powerful meaning, and the message it will communicate will be on a par with the magical incantation or curse. When he becomes angry with a playmate, he may now accuse him of being stupid. Then, if the playmate detects derision in the tone of voice used and defends himself by denying that he is stupid, the word's power is further reinforced for the boy.

And so the process goes on. We learn to associate strong emotions—hope, fear, happiness, sorrow—with word symbols. We use words to convey both meaning and feeling; we succeed; and then we begin to believe implicitly that the power is inherent in the words themselves.

To some extent, we undermine this belief at an early age by teaching our children distrust for words. We do this because our system for teaching the meaning and power of words is not completely consistent. The Santa Claus tradition, for instance, teaches the child that people older, wiser, and stronger than himself may employ words to deceive him. Then, at about the age of seven, he discovers that there is no Santa Claus; and, no matter whether he reacts with shock or disappointment or surprise, the revelation may be the first step toward permanent skepticism.

Later on, we resort to the same mechanism. We threaten the teenager with the prospect of catching cold or pneumonia if he goes outdoors without his coat. He listens to our admonition and decides to test our wisdom. Because he does not catch cold, much less pneumonia, he decides that the Santa Claus routine has been used again. In school, too, his teacher tells him, "If you cheat, I will fail you." The young student, perhaps striving with all his ability to live up to his parents' concept of him as bright and capable, learns that the teacher is not all-seeing or all-knowing and that he can successfully deceive others while also satisfying his parents' demands for good grades.

At last the boy grows up and goes to work. He is told that if he works hard and displays promise, the sky is the limit as far as promotion is concerned. He observes, however, that relatives and fraternity brothers of well-placed company officers are more likely to be promoted than anyone else and that sometimes hard work not only goes unnoticed but may even be termed poor. His cynicism begins to harden. He decides that phrases such as "a fair day's work" and "honest in all things" are used primarily to control him so that the purposes of others may be served. With Eliza Doolittle he says, "Words, words, words! I've had enough of words! Now show me!"

To be sure, words never completely lose their magic. We rely on them to communicate with one another, to know one another, and to solve our deepest and most pressing problems. They are efficient and necessary tools of our culture. However, we often teach people to become unresponsive because we try to "fool" them with words. Perhaps we have tried to make language do the job when much more was needed. We have overused words so much that now only actions will suffice. We have cried "Wolf!" "Fire!" "Bless you!" and "Curse you!" so often for mere dramatic effect that some of the power these terms once had to influence us has seeped away.

## The Age-Old Problem

What we face here is the question of social control and influence. We use words as a means of getting people to do what we want them to do, and our early efforts succeed. Then we begin to feel a sense of personal power and a fascination with the impact of our words. We experiment with words to deceive other people as we have been deceived. Or, if our conscience will not let us deceive anyone intentionally, we use simple distortions or small errors.

A man who has never before run a forklift climbs into the driver's seat and turns the switch as he has seen others do. A friend shouts, "You can't do that! You don't know how to drive a forklift!" He automatically responds, "Yes, I do!" His words are only a partial distortion of the truth. He has seen others turn the switch and drive the vehicle off many times, and he is aware of each element in operating it. But he is unlikely to be aware of the machine's limitations, which can be appreciated only through experience in driving it. The fact is that he has never driven a forklift before yet can say he knows how. If his friend does not sense the deception, an unsupervised driving lesson may take place.

Similarly, a manager tells an employee, "You are not qualified for promotion to that opening." The employee almost automatically replies, "I *am* qualified." Manager and employee use words in an attempt to influence each other's behavior. The manager wants the employee to accept without rancor the fact that he will not be promoted, and the employee wants the manager to reconsider and promote him. Emotions run high, words fly thick and fast, exact meanings are lost, and the game of "Let's see what I can talk you into doing" is under way.

This is one of the most serious problems confronting the manager in his relations with his subordinates. The game of who-can-talk-whom-into-doing-what is so thoroughly ingrained in the behavior of both manager and employee that few people are able to break away from it. Each person is absorbed in using words to induce the desired behavior in his adversary while at the same time preventing that adversary from influencing him. The function of communicating is almost totally lost; instead, all effort is directed toward influencing and controlling others. The manager tries to get what he wants from the employee, the employee tries to get what he wants from the company, parents demand obedience from children, children insist on having their own way—and the fight is on.

## Controlling and Being Controlled

Efforts to control other people through the medium of words reach their zenith in the application of techniques such as brainwashing and hypnosis, and the phenomenon of hypnosis itself is enough to convince many people of the magic of words.

What happens in both activities is that one person, consciously or otherwise, permits himself to be dominated by another. In hypnosis, the subject cooperates with the hypnotist. In brainwashing, the subject is weakened, threatened, or punished until he loses the will to resist. At that point, the tormenter can make his subject say almost anything. There is no magic in these procedures, however—they are closely documented and can be described in considerable detail. The ability of one person to brainwash or hypnotize another proves nothing except mastery of the techniques for dominating others and a willingness to keep looking until a suitable candidate is found. If the subject cooperates or can be tormented and weakened into submission, the process can be carried to completion.

The bald attempt to use words to control behavior is likely to be met with fierce resistance. In a democracy, the typical reaction is, "You can't tell me what to do; this is a free country." Put a half-dozen businessmen in a room without any instruction as to which one is the leader or how the group is to organize itself, and each man will spend the first several days proving to everyone else that he can't be told what to do. Ambitious, competitive people quickly learn to avoid being controlled by mere words. Having learned, they may spend much of their time thereafter thwarting any attempts to get them to behave in a specific way.

A special concept of "reverse psychology" has been developed in which people work out elaborate schemes to convince a person to do something in hopes that he will do the direct opposite. But this stratagem is eventually revealed, and the discovery frequently leads to highly unpredictable or erratic behavior *as an ultimate means* of preventing control.

Deception, half-truths, irresponsibility—these are commonly used tactics in the attempt to manipulate the behavior of others through the medium of language. But the result of playing the communication game in this way is great impairment of the efficacy of communication—plus the very real possibility of warping or destroying the utility of words for straightforward communication at another time. Both are potentially serious in terms of today's world.

Over and over, people are led to entertain high hopes and expectations. Over and over they are disappointed. Not only do advertising and public relations people seek to induce certain attitudes about products, services, and certain behavior patterns, but we find public relations firms consciously creating false images of opposing political candidates. More and more a long-suffering citizenry is realizing that many utterances which appear in the form of advertising, speeches, and releases are "managed news."

Although we can be sure that managed news is nothing new, it has recently become an issue of considerable concern and even hot debate. People in growing numbers are becoming aware of the cynicism with which many messages are directed toward them. They are beginning to sense that the purpose of these messages is to direct their behavior, and they are learning that it may be in their own best interests not to respond. What would happen if everybody lost trust in all advertisers and—worse—all public officials? Will we one day see real changes in news reporting and advertising as well as in the statements of politicians and public officials because managed information is no longer effective? Such a prediction probably is unrealistic. There is no doubt, however, that much distortion is taking place in mass communication today and that the response is likely to be increasingly erratic.

All methods of using words to direct and control behavior are interesting in their own right. The danger lies in resorting to them unknowingly—and with dire results. Frequently, the well-intentioned industrial manager or political leader falls into communication traps simply because he is unaware that his tactics are much the same ones that "con" artists traditionally have used to take advantage of their "marks."

## Influencing with Information

The basic technique for activating behavior is to provide an individual with factual information about an opportunity. For example, you may say, "It's possible to get rich these days in the commodities market." Whether the possibility is one in a billion or one in two is beside the point; the existence of the opportunity can be shown by naming specific people who *have* gotten rich in the commodities market. Similarly, it's likely that back before the turn of the century somebody remarked, "It should be possible to put an internal combustion engine in a buggy and eliminate the need for the horse." At the time there was probably a good deal of dispute as to the odds of such a possibility's becoming a reality, much less a *practical* reality, but someone did recognize it—to the consternation of the disbelievers.

A person can, of course, work out the facts for himself without being apprised of an opportunity by someone else. A classic example is Columbus, who came to the conclusion that if the world was round, it must be possible to reach the Indies by sailing west. Having examined the evidence and found it impelling, Columbus was ready to move on to the next step in his search for a trade route to the Indies across the Atlantic Ocean.

There are, in fact, endless examples of information's eliciting action. When it became known that the atom could be split, this suggested opportunities for the development of the atomic electric power plant and scores of other likely and unlikely applications. And so it is in business and industry: To advise a diving-equipment manufacturer that the U.S. Navy is interested in proposals for deep-sea diving vehicles; to tell an employee that if he acquires skill in computer programming he can obtain a better classification and more pay; to advise a vice president in charge of marketing of a new use for a company by-product—all these are methods of pointing out existing opportunities through the medium of relatively pure information—provided that the advice is correct and given without self-interest.

In day-to-day life, communication is used time and again to pass along information about previously unknown opportunities. Answering a friend's question about the employee-run credit union tells him he can borrow money from a source other than a bank or finance company. Advising the high school senior that a certain college offers a bachelor's degree in all the liberal arts fields, plus teaching credentials, but that it does not have an engineering curriculum, informs him what opportunities do and do not exist there. Telling a driver he must conform to traffic regulations or be penalized shows him ways in which he may avoid punishment or court it. Reminding one's husband that he can earn time-and-a-half for working beyond his regular shift gives him the choice of earning extra money or forgoing those earnings. The transfer of information, in short, is a highly important use of communication.

When a dispute arises as to what opportunities exist for a business, a family, or an individual, the best course is to stick to the facts. However, facts are not always as plentiful as we would like. In some cases we have no choice but to deal with opinion and probability, because firm facts on which to base our action simply do not exist. For example, what are the qualities of the ideal secretary for Lou Fraser? We can only answer, "It depends!" If Lou is a 25-year-old junior executive who believes that having an attractive blonde outside his office will improve his status, he is likely to describe the ideal secretary in terms of her appearance. The employment manager, on the other hand, may describe her in terms of skills and experience, and

Lou's wife may come up with still another set of specifications. Depending upon immediate need, point of view, experience, and ability to analyze the problem systematically and objectively, a wide variety of solutions may be offered.

In much the same way, we answer crucial questions without firm facts: What career should I undertake? What are the basic qualifications for the managerial position we are trying to fill? What should be the scope of our business? Should we merge with the XYZ Corporation? Most such vital questions have to do with issues about which information is incomplete. The final decision must often depend largely on a reasonably accurate assessment of possibilities which are not fully assessable and on individual preferences.

When facts are not sufficient to describe existing opportunities with any precision, the matter of directing and controlling behavior arises. We are now dealing with opportunities which are not clear-cut and which, in popular terminology, must be "sold." If we are to convince an employee that higher production is necessary and desirable or sell a customer on the superiority of our product, we must somehow dramatize the information we provide in order to influence him toward the course of action we want him to take.

## The Three Techniques

Three basic techniques are used to increase the likelihood of eliciting a desired response even when the reason for action is not clear-cut:

1. *Out-and-out twisting, distorting, or invention of facts*—one of the oldest and most elementary techniques for enhancing the attractiveness of otherwise ambiguous opportunities.
2. *Withholding information;* that is, failing to tell the individual about any details that do not support the case—both those that weaken it and those that reveal opportunities other than the ones the speaker wants the listener to pursue.
3. *Distortion of the probabilities*—the time-honored technique of suggesting that something is more (or less) likely to occur than it may actually be.

*Lying.* The invention or gross misinterpretation of facts is as ancient as communication itself. In its subtlest form, the lie takes the form of a bluff. The poker player tries to convince his adversaries through a display of confidence that he can meet and raise the bets at hand, that he has an ace in the hole to go with the two on the board, and that he can top the man who has three tens showing. In the culture of poker playing, however, bluffing is accepted and, once recognized, is dealt with directly. Typically, when another player matches the bluffer's raise he does so with the statement, "It's worth the money to keep you honest." It is clearly a good investment to learn whether your adversary is an effective liar.

Lying is used by the supervisor who tells you that your idea is worthless or has been used many times before, but later presents it to higher management or to the patent office as his own. It is used by the car dealer who sells the new-looking trade-in with the cracked block or the ambitious executive who undercuts his rival by reporting, falsely, that the latter has made disrespectful comments about the boss.

Where people do not have direct access to the facts, the possibilities of lying increase. If only two people witness an event and describe it in mutually exclusive terms, it is usually obvious that one of them is lying, though which of the two is the liar is hard to determine. At the very least, some gross distortion of the truth can be assumed. In many cases, of course, only one report of an incident is available. There is then no direct conflict of evidence—only the unsupported statement of a single individual whose word we do not know whether to trust or discount. When an important decision rests on such an unsupported statement and it is possible to obtain the facts, we should never hesitate to do so, even at the risk of offending the person who made the report. This is especially true if the potential costs of making an error are high. If, on the other hand, little is involved, we can always test the individual's truthfulness—like the poker player who calls his opponent's bluff to keep him honest.

*Withholding information.* Lying is at least straightforward; if the liar is found out, we know how to deal with him from then on. Withholding information, in contrast, poses quite a different problem. We may be presented with only some of the facts, although the omission of significant and important details may influence our decision and subsequent action.

The employee who tells his boss, "I have to handle some legal affairs tomorrow," and requests the day off with pay may be stating a clear and unassailable fact. But he may be omitting the pertinent fact that he intends to spend most of the day looking for a new job. If this is the case, he is withholding relevant information. Should the boss be at all suspicious, he may ask, "Do you intend to spend the entire day on legal matters?" The employee then has the choice of lying, continuing to withhold information, or telling the whole truth. To answer the question without actually lying, he may resort to evasion. "No, but if I have any time left, I should go to the dentist." The boss who is still not content with this explanation may persist further. In that event, the employee may be able to avoid lying and continue to provide only partial or irrelevant information until the boss gives up. More likely, he will be less skilled with words than his boss and, finally, will break down and either tell the truth or resort to a lie.

Should the boss find out later that the employee has indeed gone looking for a new job during his paid day off, he may accuse him of lying. Such an accusation will, of course, be denied if the employee has answered his boss's questions "truthfully" without volunteering any information that might prove adverse to his case. All he can really be accused of is a lack of frankness and openness about his real purposes and motives in taking the day off.

A similar lack of frankness may characterize the person who feels he has been taken advantage of through someone's persuasive efforts. He too may be inclined, not to lie, but to withhold essential information. Take the district sales manager who has been persuaded, against his will, to accept a higher quota for his territory than the facts warrant and who then conceals from headquarters the forthcoming introduction of a competitive product. If the sales chief tries to blame the district man for the unexpected loss of business, the latter can describe what "actually" happened and often make the accuser seem inept at verbal exchange.

In a fiercely competitive environment, it can be naive to let all one's resources, opportunities, and intentions become known. Keeping one's competitors in the dark about plans and policies is a strategy clearly intended to make it impossible for them to determine your goals and intentions. If the action you plan to take is unknown to someone who does not want you to succeed, it is difficult for him to erect barriers against you. Thus companies are naturally reluctant to reveal information about promotional plans or new products. Quarterbacks try to make it difficult for the opposing team to know what play is coming, and pitchers do their best to keep the batter off guard and unprepared for the next pitch. In wartime, it is treason to give the enemy information about size and deployment of troops or details about new equipment.

In a less dramatic vein, the mere possession of information often gives its possessor a distinct advantage which he may lose if he releases the information too freely. The boss's secretary, for instance, may acquire prestige and influence far beyond her formal status merely because she has information that is of great concern to others and may be prevailed upon to reveal it if she is "treated right." In a large organization, moreover, not only is it often difficult to get one department to disclose information to another unless it can be convinced that doing so will not affect it adversely, but people who are in possession of needed information frequently exact a price for its release. For the straightforward withholding of information is not the only important maneuver in organizational and individual strategy; the provision of information for value received also is widely used.

Holding back information, although a second cousin to the lie and often confused with it, is in reality a manipulatory tactic. It is a way of gaining or maintaining an advantage so as to achieve one's own ends through others. It is inscrutability put to selfish ends.

*Distortion of probabilities.* Between lying and withholding information is to be found the remaining tactic: the art of making the long shot look like a sure thing. This is distortion of the probabilities of an event's occurrence. Sometimes it is very nearly a lie; at other times it is merely a suggestion of a cause-and-effect relationship which is made in the hope that the listener will swallow it whole.

Examples of this tactic are ubiquitous. Modern-day advertisements imply that this mouthwash or that deodorant will turn the tide of your personal popularity or transform your romantic life or that a shirt, tie, suit, or bourbon will make you a man of distinction. All overstate the probabilities with the intention of influencing behavior —in these instances, buyer behavior.

But advertisers are not alone in the use of this tactic. The mother who insists, "If you go near the water, you'll fall in and drown," is equally guilty of overstating the probabilities. So, too, is the employer who tells employees, "If you vote for the union, we'll be unable to stay competitive in our market," and the union organizer who says, "If you don't have a union, they can throw you out on the street any time."

Overstating either the rewards or the penalties inherent in opportunities for action is perhaps the most widely used technique for controlling, directing, or manipulating behavior. It is more common than withholding facts because it takes less skill. It is preferable to both withholding information and lying in that, if one is found out, no more is at stake than a reputation for exaggeration. Beyond these concerns, overstatement is popular because it goes to the heart of the matter: It plays directly on the hopes, fears, and needs of people in persuading them to pursue specific goals. A door-to-door salesman may gain entrance to a home by declaring that he is making a survey; he withholds the information that his true purpose is to make a sale. Once inside, the technique he is most likely to use is distortion of the probabilities that his product will improve the housewife's ability to manage more efficiently.

However, the overstatement or gross exaggeration of probabilities has a built-in reality test. This is particularly so when the listener takes the action suggested by the message. The purchaser of the deodorant, mouthwash, or bourbon whose love life changes not in the least; the employees who reject the union and don't lose their jobs (or who accept the union and are laid off anyway); the housewife who is no more efficient than she was before—all these people find out that the probabilities are nowhere near what they were said to be. The assertions having been readily tested and found wanting, the communicators' manipulatory intent is unmasked.

When probabilities are distorted to the extent that they are in our society, a measure of public cynicism soon sets in. There is evidence all around us now that this is reaching epidemic proportions.

Despite lying, the withholding of information, and the distortion of probabilities, many kernels of useful information await the listener. As long as we communicate enough, we are bound to inform, if only by accident. Furthermore, informative communication is essential if we are to expand the opportunities available to people. However, an important question is: Can we wait until our audience has learned to separate the informational wheat from the manipulatory chaff? In the past, legislation has been the tool designed to control the would-be manipulator. If we cannot learn to understand the consequences of manipulatory communication, we will probably have to endure some kind of external control in the future.

# 3

*Information Processing*

*and Reality Testing*

THE DEVELOPMENT OF MANAGERS for modern organizations, business and otherwise, takes two distinct directions, depending upon the existing pressures. Managers attack a job either by solving problems logically and systematically or by fighting fires. In the first instance, their principal concern is with the facts they hope to use in arriving at a rational, sensible solution. Managers who take the fire-fighting approach, however, use every conceivable kind of available information, mixing it together in an artful fashion to permit a summary decision.

The typical mathematician, business management graduate, engineer, physicist, or physical scientist follows the first approach because he inclines toward dealing with any problem logically, systematically, and scientifically. In contrast, the practical man (often without a college education) who came up through the ranks, the liberal arts graduate, the psychologist, and the sociologist all tend toward a more artful and emotional style of problem solving. In the process of learning how to identify problems by classes, the self-taught man feels his way through each one and reaches a decision about its solution more on the basis of his gut reaction than any logical analysis. He probably does so for two reasons: First, the pressures of the job require that he react to problems rather than solve them; second, his lack of formal higher education compels him to use his practical abilities to their fullest—which means that if he is to get ahead at all, he cannot afford the luxury of being absolutely, logically, and completely certain of every solution.

The typical social scientist or liberal arts graduate is in much the same predicament. As a matter of preference he probably approaches problem solving from a more sophisticated point of view based on an overall predilection for ingenuity and an emotional sense of the correct solution rather than on a lack of concern for tangible facts. Indeed, these were probably his principal reasons for choosing his field of study to begin with.

This two-way classification of logical/emotional problem solving is very useful. Some managers use both; in fact, the most effective manager has developed his ability to shift gears and apply either the logical or the emotional approach as the situation demands. When the risks and costs of failure are high, he accepts nothing less than solid facts as the basis of his decisions. When real-time responsiveness is critical, he unleashes his emotional problem-solving capabilities. Whenever possible, he solves a problem both ways, using each method as a check on the other.

## Objective or Subjective Reality?

It is the rare individual who is capable of employing both methods of problem solution with equal skill. Typically, a manager begins by following his natural inclination to use one or the other approach and sticks with it. Which is the more comfortable will probably depend largely on whether he is interested principally in the external, objective world or the internal, subjective world.

*External and objective.* We may call objective those elements of nature which we observe directly and which repeat themselves with a fair degree of consistency under similar conditions. If the air inside a thin metal container is heated and the container is then sealed and allowed to cool, it will collapse. Every time these conditions occur, whether by accident or by design, the result will be the same—owing to a fact of nature which has made possible not only the experimental collapsing of tin cans but also the development of the steam engine.

Some physical facts apply to people with the same degree of reliability. If an infant cries because he is hungry, he will stop crying when he is fed. If a child is consistently denied warmth and love, he will grow up emotionally and socially incompetent. If an elderly man trips and loses his balance, he will fall. These are cause-and-effect relationships which we may depend on to be highly consistent. For the most part, they describe the realities of our world. They are *objective* realities.

The advantage of dealing with objective realities is that they are not easily disputed. In the event of disagreement, a cause-and-effect relationship can be demonstrated directly. Argument therefore carries with it a low level of risk; there is little ambiguity or confusion.

Most objective facts are in the realm of the physical sciences. Chemistry and physics with their applied arm, engineering, enjoy something of a corner on physical facts. A few reliable cause-and-effect sequences may exist in the fields of psychology, sociology, and economics, but generally these areas are subject to far less certainty.

*Internal and subjective.* A human being who is hungry will generally seek food. But many overweight individuals intentionally forgo eating as a means of reducing, even though they may suffer hunger pangs as a consequence. In the main, people avoid pain or discomfort —yet many women have been known to wear tight shoes in the interest of fashion. In the main, too, people avoid situations that might be physically harmful to them—yet firemen dash into burning buildings to rescue trapped occupants and soldiers march into battle in the face of flying bullets.

The only thing we can be sure of with respect to people is that, given half a chance, they will upset our predictions about their behavior. There is no such thing as a totally reliable cause-and-effect prediction about the human animal, who has few natural or instinctive limitations on his range of behavior. When it comes to natural morality, the wolf has it over man; two wolves in battle will fight until the one that can endure no more turns his soft underflank to his adversary. No wolf will take advantage of this opening to destroy his opponent; whereas, given the opportunity to destroy his adversary so easily, a man may show mercy or he may be pitiless. Every human being must learn which behavior is preferable to him; there is no natural restraint on him in favor of either. Just because he has few physiological limits on his behavior, however, man has boundless potential for exploring a variety of behavior patterns. He may do or try virtually anything; his only limitations are his natural or learned needs and his conditioned fears.

The condition of man described here is the foundation of what we will call "subjective reality." This is a good deal less reliable and less predictable than external reality; however, because in conjunction with this high degree of unpredictability, man has infinite capacity for accomplishment and creativity, subjective reality is as crucial as objective reality—if not more so—in determining how a person will behave under any set of circumstances. It is frequently impossible to know what he is going to do in a given situation unless we ask him how he feels about it. Thus becoming aware of his subjective reaction to external reality is the critical variable in predicting what he will do.

Our need to know how people feel is often greater than we realize. For example, an investor was once heard to say that the annual reports of the corporation whose stock offerings he was considering were useless to him: "What I need to know is how the people who work in the organization feel about it." This man has obviously concluded that the perceptions and motivations of the employees are at least as important as the financial data about their company. Certainly, such data seem essential in predicting future changes in organizational health or growth.

The most important form of subjective reality is our own individual experiences and feelings. It is a matter of introspection and of trying to determine "what I am." The individual who, through exploration and experimentation, learns to understand and appreciate himself has begun to fathom the depths of subjective reality which exists for every human being. Examining, exploring, and defining the potential which is "myself" is therefore one of the most important things anyone does.

*The Tendency Toward Polarization*

People, as we have said, have a natural tendency to polarize toward either logical or emotional problem solving. Some people enjoy introspection and subjective reality. Others reject the realm of opinion and subjectivity in favor of external, objective reality. This is probably a function of chance successes in one realm or the other as the individual matures. If, for instance, a man is highly successful as a youngster in the academic world of words and ideas, he is likely to be attracted to the subjective side of reality. He finds that he can quickly develop the skills necessary for effective human relations and deal successfully with other people. His subjective capabilities serve him well; therefore, he appreciates and explores them further. On the other hand, the student who has difficulty with concepts, but who finds it easy to deal with physical objects, spatial relationships, or mathematics, enjoys his first successes and continues to make progress in areas where clear-cut answers and highly reliable cause-and-effect relationships prevail.

As the tendency to polarize grows, any difficulties or failures centering about the opposite pole drive the individual more strongly toward the pole that has already attracted him. It is in this way that he develops a preference for history and languages and a dislike for mathematics and the physical sciences, or vice versa. Such a bent is not accidental or capricious; it has a basis in the nature of our world: Simply as a matter of chance, it is easy for a person to become effective at learning and employing the many cause-and-effect relationships of the physical sciences or, alternatively, to become more proficient at dealing with loose verbal and ideational concepts such as those inherent in history, language, and the liberal arts. The resulting polarization frequency follows an individual throughout his lifetime. As a result we find, not infrequently, that the engineer instinctively evaluates a marketing report as "just a lot of unsupported opinions," whereas the marketing man reacts with the comment, "He just doesn't understand the problem. He thinks you can write a formula to solve it."

The dichotomy, furthermore, is encouraged by the structure of college programs: The student who is committed to a physics curriculum learns to focus on firm, scientific solutions of problems. In contrast, the student who is taking a degree in philosophy becomes enamored of verbal concepts and ideas as a way of dealing with and understanding his world.

## The Integrated Approach

We need not labor the differences between subjective and objective realities. Differences do exist, but there is nothing inherent in man that requires him to concentrate on the one and turn his back on the other. Indeed, the ability to deal with both realities and to solve problems competently in both these spheres of human affairs is a most valuable skill.

The sciences, of course, emphasize the importance of facts, and they will undoubtedly continue to do so. On the other hand, practitioners in such fields as medicine and business management are more likely to stress the importance of dealing effectively with the problem at hand, regardless of whether they have enough facts. The effective manager should strive to become proficient in both approaches. The various techniques available today for application to management development programs can be rather neatly divided into those that emphasize rational problem solving, those that emphasize emotional competence in dealing with problems, and those that integrate the two techniques.

Approaches to management development which emphasize rationality in reaching decisions call for pinpointing facts that determine accurate cause-and-effect sequences and achieving an unassailably accurate judgment. These approaches contrast strongly with the currently popular sensitivity-training, T-group, or laboratory-training effort and business-games approach to developing managers in which managers are sent off for days or weeks of training designed to help them probe their innermost resources, to learn what impact they have on other people, and to achieve a greater understanding of the dynamics of group interaction. The best evidence we have indicates that such training engenders an increased sensitivity to the concerns and needs of others and that it helps managers learn to use the opinions of others as sources of information and as basic data upon which to base decisions.

The business-games approach to management development places much less emphasis on group dynamics or logic and more on learning how to classify situations correctly and react to them appropriately. In the game setting, the manager is presented with far more variables than he can deal with logically in the time allotted and he is required to handle them subjectively in achieving sound business decisions as the situation permits. If he learns anything from business games, it is how to program his emotions so that he can react immediately and directly to problems and make sensible decisions on the basis of limited information.

Anyone who is aware of a "weak suit" in his own deck of talents should make use of the appropriate course of training from among those just listed.


*Neither the One nor the Other*


Our basic problem is thus a familiar one; it is the problem of learning how to deal most efficiently with the information available to us in reaching decisions.

Some people prefer the logical to the emotional approach, or the emotional to the logical, in problem solving because of chance successes or failures they have had with one or the other in the early stages of learning. They may have made a firm commitment to one particular academic discipline. This seems a natural state of affairs; people tend to favor conditions in which they feel capable and competent. The point should be made, however, that neither approach is sufficient in itself to meet all the problems of management decision making in modern organizations. Both capacities must be developed in managers and employees alike.

Typically, the manager of a shop or of a manufacturing operation who is under great pressure to achieve a high level of productivity and efficiency learns the emotional approach early in his development. The industrial engineer, on the other hand, must usually justify his recommendations on unimpeachably rational grounds; therefore, he tends to start from a base of highly skilled, logical problem solving. At some stage, both probably will compete for the position of manager of the total operation. Who is to say which is the better qualified? The only accurate answer is that *neither is fully prepared* for all the problems he will have to face as over-all manager.

The manager who is a good, rational problem solver needs to

become more artful; the manager who is already an artful problem solver needs added competence in the systematic, scientific solution of problems. Until both approaches are mastered, it is unlikely that either man will be able to appreciate every problem fully or cope with it effectively.

## Gearing Communication to the Audience

What does this have to do with communication? A great deal. Successful communication with another individual is difficult, if not impossible, unless the speaker knows whether the listener is an emotional or a logical problem solver. Some people will respond to feelings, opinions, and ideas and feel comfortable in doing so; others will accept only information that has been stripped down to the bare bones.

The reasons for this are simple: The logical problem solver generally does not feel at home with emotional issues and personal opinions. He has chosen the logical approach as a way of protecting himself from his own ineptitude in handling unstructured situations. The emotional problem solver, in contrast, has chosen the opposite approach because of his natural skill in dealing with conceptualizations of issues and a concurrent ineptitude in seeking logical, scientific solutions. With the logical problem solver, communication must be deliberate and objective; with the emotional problem solver, it should be artful, highly conceptualized, and verbally attractive.

To be effective, in other words, the communicator should know how his audience processes the information he transmits.

Most people have both strengths and weaknesses in information processing. The average individual trusts his reactions to situations that do not involve intense emotions, but distrusts them when feelings run high. He is willing to go along with a logical solution of a problem he understands, but he is highly suspicious of logical formulations that exceed his level of sophistication.

Communication itself may be pitched at one or more of four specific emotional/logical levels. These are:

1. Fear-based emotional responses.
2. Need-based emotional responses.

3. Logical disciplines that provide data or facts.
4. Logical disciplines that provide confirmation or testing of the truth.

*Fear-oriented communications.* When we lack information, most of us make complex decisions principally on the basis of our emotional reactions. The most prevalent of these reactions is fear, which can be—and frequently is—an all-pervasive quality that dominates individual behavior. True, behavior based on fear is occasionally effective—the same fear that immobilizes one man in the face of danger causes another to snatch a child from the path of an approaching automobile. But, however the direction and quality of the response may vary, behavior based on fear is always intense. As a result, fear is one of the most important factors in human behavior.

Think of the varying responses that can be precipitated by

- ✧ Fear of disappointing family or friends.
- ✧ Fear of being rejected by friends or by members of the opposite sex.
- ✧ Fear of losing a job.
- ✧ Fear of offending people in authority.
- ✧ Fear of being taken advantage of.
- ✧ Fear of pain.

A good deal of human behavior is, in fact, traceable to these simple fear situations. The fear of being rejected probably keeps more people from a close, warm, intimate relationship with other human beings than anything else. Human beings deny themselves opportunities and pleasures more because of their fears than for any other reason.

When we talk of irrational behavior, we generally mean fear-motivated behavior. The man who jumps from the sixth floor of a burning building while a ladder is being raised to rescue him, the employee who quits out of fear of being fired, and the child who refuses to go to school because he is afraid he will fail a test—all are typical examples of the debilitating effects of fear, panic-faced fear, rooted in poorly defined cause-and-effect relationships, of the sort that causes a drowning man to flounder and thrash instead of inflating his life jacket.

To say that some of the poorest problem solving is done in response to fear is not to say that fear is a useless emotion. Our lives may depend on our being afraid to step in front of a speeding car or light a match near a gas tank. Many hazards confront us, and a good number of them—certainly those we are likely to encounter in our daily life and work—can be defined in terms of the likelihood of their occurrence and the degree of risk they involve. But emotions are not always rational or logical. The man who knows his work is good may nevertheless be anxious about his boss's evaluation of it, and in an effort to assuage his anxiety he may light a cigarette without regard for the possible effect of smoking on his health. In few instances are the probabilities of having our fears realized ever confirmed clearly, but this point is worth making: Some low-probability hazards create intense anxiety and fear in us, whereas others whose probability is high seem not to affect us at all.

Merely to write off these fears serves no purpose. They are part of that very important realm we have described as subjective reality. To communicate with a person effectively, we must know what his fears are; they act as powerful filters on his ability to perceive the subjective or factual information available to him. The man who is terrified of losing his job has difficulty hearing messages that are unrelated to this fear. He is wrapped up in listening for cues confirming his belief that his job is in jeopardy; he has ears for little else. He may not even hear messages aimed at assuring him of his job security, or he may distort them to fit his fears. Or, if the prospect of the loss of his job is intolerable, he may overlook evidence that many jobs in the organization are in danger because the company cannot compete in its market, or he may misinterpret that same evidence so as to block out the threatening message.

Messages that contradict a conviction may also go unheeded lest the conviction be proved false. The man who believes his boss does not like him will be all but impossible to convince that he is wrong. The employee who is convinced that piecework is a way of increasing production without increasing wages is not likely to hear the arguments in favor of a piecework plan. The wife who is devoted to her husband will hear no criticism of him; the partisan who is committed to a political party and a candidate will hear nothing uncomplimentary to either; and the man who has just paid $6,000 for an automobile will hear nothing about its technical deficiencies.

Simply because people's fears get in the way of their receiving incoming messages, the most carefully prepared communication may have no result if it fails to take into account the fears of the people it is intended to reach. Consider radio transmission as an analogy. It does no good to transmit sound at frequencies of 4,000 cycles per second if the receiver will accept nothing above 2,000 cycles. In other words, high-fidelity transmission is useless unless there is high-fidelity reception at the other end. Unfortunately, much of our communicating at its subtlest is akin to transmitting at the wrong frequency. Unless we can assess the receiving capabilities and limitations of our audience, our communication may well go for naught.

*Need-based response.* That human beings have needs is a truism that hardly bears repeating, but the nature of these needs is subject to endless, fascinating debate. Abraham Maslow has hypothesized that man has various levels of needs, beginning with the physiological and progressing through the more sophisticated, including the needs for security and for autonomy, and ending up with the highest order of need: for self-realization or self-actualization. At the lowest level, man barely satisfies his physical requirements; at the highest, he realizes his fullest potential as a human being.

Maslow and others further suggest that the hierarchy of needs can be used to explain the motivation of human beings; the theory is that a satisfied need does not serve to motivate. The affluent man, with a secure job and all the creature comforts he wants, is not moved by the prospect of securing food, domestic comfort, or job security. He is more likely to be concerned with achieving some degree of self-direction, autonomy, and self-respect. In fact, he may even be willing to sacrifice a measure of his security in order to gain greater self-respect. Hence we see that in order to communicate effectively with someone we must know the level of need at which he is currently operating.

An alternate theory of human needs, proposed by Robert Ardrey in *The Territorial Imperative*, suggests that there are basically only two needs: (1) the need for physical and emotional *security* and (2) the need for physical and emotional *stimulation*. Although this theory is still in the developmental stages, the idea behind it is impelling. There are many situations in which the central motives of human beings seem to revolve around a conflict between the need to be secure and the need to receive stimulation and excitement from the environment. There is evidence, for instance, that infants need to be fondled and caressed in order to survive. It has been shown that children in foundling homes who are not picked up and petted regularly have a higher mortality rate than those who have normal physical contact with parents and other adults. Thus, it would seem that, without the physical stimulation that conveys a message of support, life is not worth living to at least some children. Indeed, when motivation is viewed from the perspective of security and stimulation, it is not so strange that married couples fight or that employees go out on strike. The most attractive adjustments seem to be those that simultaneously provide both the most intense excitement and the greatest degree of security.

Fascinating though it may be to discuss theories of human needs, it is not entirely relevant. Most employees are controlled, not by appealing to their needs, but by reminding them of their fears. Although this state of affairs has been decreasing during the past few decades, the typical individual is still dominated more by self-imposed fears than by internal needs. Making the transition from basic physiological and psychological needs to self-realization and self-actualization can be accomplished only if the individual examines the subjective reality of his own personality and conquers his irrational and emotional fears. And, to deal effectively with these fears and to use genuine needs as determiners of human action, he must achieve a degree of mastery over both objective and subjective realities.

*Logical disciplines providing facts.* It has not been many years since the seasoned pilot prided himself on his ability to fly his plane by the seat of his pants. This kind of aerodynamics was no doubt exciting, but the pride which it prompted came at a high price in life and limb.

There will always be thrill seekers who are eager to engage in activities whose risks are real and imminent, and we should not be unnecessarily smug about criticizing their tendency to take such risks. After all, it has made possible many significant advances in automobile racing, flying, and even the exploration of space. In fields where human capability is being pushed to and beyond recognized limits, risk taking is essential.

Behavior of this sort is, of course, based entirely on emotional motivation. It certainly is not logical.

Though we are not all daredevils, however, we all must solve problems that involve some risk. To minimize the risk, we must seek the safest solution—the one which takes into account all the relevant facts. When facts are available or can be obtained, they should generally be studied before making the decision. Why "generally"? Because not all decisions *have* to be based on fact.

As an illustration, when the demand for a given product—say, a hula hoop—is high, it doesn't make a great deal of difference whether most of the hula hoops produced are red, green, or yellow. The urge to have any hula hoop at all will probably overcome any disappointments about color and will permit the easy sale of the entire output. Under these circumstances, it will *not* be profitable to conduct market research on customer color preferences; *the cost of obtaining the facts would far exceed the benefits of having them.* In other words, the costs of any error in color-preference predictions will probably be wholly offset by the high level of market demand, so that errors will be tolerable.

On the other hand, an error may mean the difference between economic success and failure for a manufacturer of cosmetics. Producing a shade of lipstick that few women would use will leave the company with an unsalable supply of expensive merchandise. In a highly competitive market, where color differentiation has become one of the principal determinants of customer acceptance or rejection, it would be foolish not to find out what lipstick colors women want. The potential cost of a poor decision is so high that conducting market research—that is, obtaining the facts about customer preference—is not only feasible but economically essential.

To sum up, then, facts are comparable to any other product or service: Each has its own marginal utility, depending on business needs and circumstances. Sometimes it costs more to obtain facts than to make a poor decision. In such situations, it is only sensible managerial judgment to take the risks involved and to make the best decision possible in the absence of hard facts. In other instances, facts are essential no matter what the cost of obtaining them.

A great many situations fall somewhere in the middle, where it is difficult to tell which would be more expensive: to obtain the facts or to risk making a poor decision. The answer cannot be known unless a commitment is made to obtain the facts, make more decisions on the basis of the facts and others without regard for them, and compare the results. The average hardheaded businessman, however, seldom does this. To begin with, he probably boasts that he is able to make sound decisions without relevant data, and he even finds a certain stimulation and personal satisfaction in doing so. The fact that good intuitive decision makers are relatively scarce and in high demand as managers further increases the attractiveness of bypassing the facts and making a decision without them: Possession of this skill insures continued employment.

When hard data are needed, they can be sought out and usually found. The sciences—physical, social, behavioral, and the rest—have proved equal to the task of providing specific information in areas of practical concern to managers. When the chips are down and nothing but the facts will do, more skill and effort should therefore be invested in the search for them; yet, in a highly competitive environment, fact-finding capability is often slighted in favor of intuitive decision making. As a result, when the times comes for fact finding in earnest, many organizations are incapable of acting effectively because the existing management team lacks the skill. In this respect the large corporation with one foot in the commercial marketplace and the other in the government-contract field has a great advantage: It can develop seasoned managers in *both* intuitive decision making and logical problem solving.

Even in organizations that give a great deal of attention to seeking out facts, moreover, one of the areas in which this activity is least developed has to do with what employees think, need, or fear. Too frequently, management does not know the concerns of its people. Yet, if it is worthwhile communicating with employees or, indeed, if it is critical that communication with them be successful, management must know how the employees are likely to respond to varying types of communication. More facts about the communication process itself are needed, and beyond the search for facts with which to improve the decision-making process lies the need for increasing use of purely factual communication, particularly within the business environment. Fears and needs have provided the easier route through which to influence customer and employee behavior through communication, and businessmen have made much use of those needs and fears, but in many organizations the skill of finding and communicating simple facts has been all but forgotten.

Effective communication with employees expands their horizons and points up ways in which they can meet their higher-order needs.

Fortunately, numerous opportunities exist for a dramatic increase in the factual news made available to employees—news which is relevant, stimulating, and anything but trivial.

*Confirming and testing the truth.* A drive to increase production efficiency is about to get under way in the large manufacturing component of a major corporation. For weeks the staff has been planning a special communication program—developing an elaborate system of awards and recognition, writing news copy, creating slogans, designing eye-catching symbols, and orienting management to all that will be required for smooth implementation.

On the day the campaign is to begin, the employees are called together in the parking lot. An elaborate reviewing stand, borrowed with considerable effort from the local university, has been set up so that top management may communicate by loudspeaker with the entire workforce. A band has been brought in. Stirring speeches are delivered; a special pennant is hoisted to a position immediately below the American flag; and large, multicolored bumper stickers and pins are handed out. To conclude the ceremony, an aerial display is set off, including a bomb that showers miniature promotional leaflets on the crowd.

The assembled employees, now released to return to their posts, drift toward the plant doors. A few laugh or talk boisterously, but most go back to their work quietly with a minimum of conversation. Listening, we discover that one of the flashiest slogans has already turned into a dirty joke and that there are a few cryptic, cynical taunts: "Well, I guess you'll have to get with it now, Harry, won't you?" It is clear that the communicators who planned this effort have been following the time-honored formula: "When you want to motivate a mule, you gotta get his attention first." The time and effort that went into this kick-off have gotten that attention; how much more the campaign has achieved remains to be seen.

For several weeks the campaign is kept in high gear. New posters go up nearly every day. Scores of reader-participation gimmicks are printed in the local house organ—everything from sentence completion to jingle writing. As time passes, management is still optimistic about the program—in fact, solidly behind it, at least for the moment —but where are the results? Very little seems to have happened with regard to production efficiency; if anything, scrap rates have gone up slightly, though not enough to be worrisome. There are, however, disturbing signs—epithets scribbled on the walls and a few anonymous suggestions—that the employees think the program is a lot of hokum.

"Perhaps it just takes time for something like this to take hold," suggests one manager. Everybody agrees, and the program goes for another week—still without positive results. At this point, a nationally known consultant is called in. He examines the program in detail, commends management for a highly creative effort, but can offer no reason why it is not effective. He does suggest that management, to insure the commitment of line personnel to the program, should be asked to hold group meetings at which production-efficiency problems will be described to all employees and then to hold individual discussions with every employee to work out ways of improving individual efficiency. Top management reacts instinctively: "We did that eight months ago, and it didn't do any good. In fact, productivity got worse." The consultant is undismayed; he has never known any harm to come from this approach, and he encourages a skeptical management to try the supervisory meetings and counseling sessions. Within a couple of weeks, production efficiency has begun to improve measurably. Things seem finally to have caught hold.

Sound familiar? This script has been played out many times in a great many organizations. Single, isolated communication programs are tried in the hope that one will work. Then, when things get desperate enough, a variety of techniques are combined and results at last appear. Is there a reason for this? Research has demonstrated that the promotional, hoopla phase of any communication effort often produces no positive results and may even have a negative effect on employee attitudes. It is almost as though they resented the attempt to talk them into doing what management wants. In like fashion, the isolated efforts of line managers to improve quality, cost, output, or whatever usually fail to produce results; rather, there may even be a decrease in productivity when pressure is put on employees by their immediate bosses. Put the isolated efforts together, however, and results begin to show.

Here we have what may be called a "rule of two" in the processing of information. People, so to speak, wait for confirmation of the legitimacy and seriousness of the original communication before acting on it. If this confirmation is not soon forthcoming *from some independent source*, the original communication is rejected. Once the employee becomes convinced that both management and his own boss are working toward a particular goal, he accepts that goal for himself.

It would appear that this rule applies to many situations where the message does not tap an intense need of the listener or where the call to action is not particularly impelling. In situations where the individual is either indifferent to the message or reluctant to respond to it, we may reasonably assume that he will *have* to receive confirming inputs from another source before he will take action. The new employee who hears a co-worker say that the boss treats his subordinates unfairly may merely file the information away for future reference; but, should a second informant pass along identical information, the employee may begin looking for a way to transfer out of the group. Again, the manager who appraises an employee as having trouble getting along with co-workers may question his own judgment—until a colleague points out the same quality. Only then is he likely to begin taking constructive action.

It should be emphasized that the rule of two is unconscious and passive. People do not systematically seek out double inputs. Indeed, the fact that both come by accident appears to be an important element of their credibility. The logic of the situation goes something like this: If two people speak up without prompting on behalf of Dr. Jones because they think he's good, there must be a lot more who feel the same way. Information thus obtained is more highly valued than information that is actively sought. If a man were to ask half a dozen people what they thought of Dr. Jones and get positive recommendations from two out of the six, he would probably consider this evidence much weaker than the unsolicited testimonials. Indeed, the spontaneous testimonial is greeted with almost childlike trust when it comes to determining what is fact and what is not.

This passive acceptance has two major drawbacks: First, it provides opportunity for coincidence as well as for testimonials carefully arranged to appear unrehearsed; that is, the rule of two can be achieved through prearrangement when a con man, for example, wants to get his point across. Second, the passive approach greatly restricts our chances of finding out about the world. Waiting stolidly for evidence to come in pairs so as to know how to act may mean inordinately long periods of inactivity—indeed, the evidence may never turn up.

It is at this juncture that we need to develop our skill in actively seeking out and evaluating information. Courses and books on interviewing, reference checking, and selection procedures emphasize ways to insure the reliability of information obtained about prospective employees. Many of the same procedures can be used for checking out data inputs of every sort.

From the manager's point of view, the rule of two says that a simple exhortation to employees to "work harder" is not likely to have results. It is not enough to make the needs and desires of management explicit; they must also be verified and supplemented through some second source. Thus higher management can speak to employees through group meetings, newspapers, bulletins, posters, and pamphlets as one source of data while immediate supervisors can speak on the personal level and be perceived as a second input.

This suggests that strict adherence to the hierarchical organization and channels is probably an ineffective way to communicate. Attempts to restrict communication to channels should, if the rule of two holds, create pressure for secondary sources of confirmation. In fact, we can nearly always find strong rumor circuits in any hierarchical organization, such as the military, where the flow of information is tightly restricted. These "grapevines," on the face of it, would seem to represent a waste of opportunity. Why not use them actively so that employees will accept what they hear as confirmation of the formal information presented to them through mass meetings, publications, or whatever?

The rule of two also suggests that an important function of staff people is to provide a supplementary source of information. Members who are in regular contact with employees can be either very useful or highly detrimental in this respect. Perceptive management will at all times be aware of the potential of staff communication and be sure that this potential is realized so as to insure its communications maximum effectiveness.

It should come as no surprise that employees need some method of testing the communications they receive; some useful, subjectively reliable, and acceptable way of gauging management's intent and the sincerity of its avowed purpose. The average manager will not consider an applicant for a key position unless he knows the man's strengths and weaknesses well or has a candidate who comes with the highest of recommendations from at least two independent sources. Why, then, should the successful candidate, when hired, not use the rule of two to arrive at his judgment of his new boss and the work group in which he finds himself?

## Level of Complexity

The rule of two would seem to imply that the simplest of communication efforts, the hierarchical-channel approach, is too simple to be consistently effective. This is probably true. How often, when we really want someone to believe us, do we settle for an unvarnished statement of fact? The natural inclination is to dramatize it so as to hold the listener's attention and convince him of our earnestness and sincerity. We learn early to distrust bold, unsupported assertions or declarations. We are often too sophisticated to accept the simple, honest, straightforward communication. Except when we have a powerful need to believe and act, we merely table it for further review. Only when confirmation comes along do we resurrect it. This is the least complex level of confirmation and perhaps the most prevalent.

Higher levels of complexity are possible and, when achieved, can greatly extend our ability to process and use information. Next, for example, we compare the input received with other available information. Both the source of the information and the prior reliability of that source may be relevant factors to consider in the evaluation of the input for immediate use. At this level, we might think of processing information according to two rules: First, if the information is received from someone who has proved reliable in the past, we use it. Second, if the information is received from someone whose reliability is either unknown or doubtful, we do not act on it until additional verification is available. Thus information processing is something of an either/or proposition.

The process may, of course, be continued almost indefinitely, taking into account wider spans as well as more complex, interconnecting networks of information. Technically, at least, any item of communication may be compared with any other. Many of the comparisons may be irrelevant or useless, but a few may turn out to be useful.

When our information-processing system has developed to the point where any given input can be fitted into a fairly well-integrated total picture, we have arrived at the highest level of information processing. We are now concerned with the way in which an item can be compared with a variety of previously developed sets and subsets of data. If the new item matches, we may accept it even though we doubt the reliability of the informant. If it does not, we may reject it even though it comes with the highest recommendation.

At this level, in effect, we operate on the basis of an integrated theory of what our organization and its objectives, purposes, and goals are all about, and we hold all inputs of information up to that theory as a way of evaluating them. This is one of the most effective methods of information processing. The individual who can use it well is in a position to make the soundest decisions. Whatever his status in the organization, he will probably be called on to make those decisions.

We might conceive of the organization itself as a total information-processing system. To the extent that it is set up hierarchically, information can enter at the top and go down; or, if it enters at some point below the top, it can go straight up and then be sent back down at the pleasure of top management. Information processing in the hierarchically strict organization tends to be simple and uncomplicated, but slow. If the information is confirmed (according to the rule of two) to the satisfaction of management or employees, it may be acted upon; otherwise, it may be ignored.

As the organization becomes more elaborate, however, and as more intracomponent, interfunctional communication lines are established and staff functions are encouraged to crisscross the organization, providing technical support and supplementary communication to the operating units, something akin to an optimal information-processing system may begin to develop. Then the information received can go directly to the area of the organization where it has the greatest relevance or where the greatest degree of specialization in evaluating information is available. Under these conditions, the rule of two may be superseded, and information which is not immediately confirmed by independent sources may still be acted on without delay.

A highly integrated, specialized, complex organization far exceeds the capability of any individual for effectively processing innumerable information inputs. The organization operating in this fashion can readily meet its needs for data regarding both external environment and internal conditions. Ample second and third sources of information exist, moreover, to satisfy the individual employee's rule of two. In the final analysis, it is this organization which can most reasonably be expected to combine the strengths of emotional decision making with those of objective problem analysis and solution. Through specialization and integration, the best of all arrangements is obtained for information processing and reality testing.

# 4

---◆·◆---

## *Ritualized Communication*

A COMMON IMAGE of the Middle Ages is that of the town crier, walking through the streets at night with a lantern to call the hour and a message of assurance: "One o'clock and all's well." To us, it may seem strange that the townspeople cared to be told the hour or that a man walking through darkened streets carrying a lantern could assert, without knowing what might be lurking in the shadows, that all was indeed well. It is not until we begin to think of communication as an end in itself that this sort of thing makes sense. The town crier served as a reassuring stimulus merely because of the familiar sounds he made. Much the same kind of need is satisfied in advertisements that say: "Sleep well tonight because your National Guard is on the alert."

In large measure, our ordinary communication is ritualized. When someone greets us with a hearty, "Good morning!" and we respond with, "How are you?" the real message in the exchange as a rule has little to do with the condition of the morning or the well-being of the speaker or listener. This kind of communication is actually just a ritualized form of recognition. It would be every bit as effective for the morning greetings to go something like this: "I see you there." "I see you, too." The exact phrasing is irrelevant. It could take the form of "I acknowledge you," "I hear you," or anything else recognizable as a conventional sign of recognition.

Go out to dinner one evening and you will see the same kind of thing going on. The restaurant owner or host says, "Good evening," and then, "This way, please." Thus he acknowledges you as a customer and announces that he is to be the controlling factor in deciding where you will sit and who will serve you. The waiter is completely impersonal. He takes your order, giving or withholding advice purely on the basis of his estimate of your willingness to reward him for good advice. He smiles, calls you "sir," and looks to your needs. The communication between you is of the most elementary sort; it concerns your preferences in food and drink and nothing more.

If you will watch the restaurant staff in the course of their varied duties, you will notice an expressionless and mechanical sort of communication, designed for the sole purpose of directing and coordinating activities, going on among them. If two waiters stop to chat, or if one of them has occasion to address a busboy, it is likely that they will talk unobtrusively out of the sides of their mouths. Little if anything beyond specific, predetermined information is transmitted in this kind of interaction, virtually all of which is ritualized and standardized.

Most communication between people is much the same. It is almost as if they were ships passing at sea, their conventional flags flying to identify themselves and their mission. In such an encounter, there need be no real concern for the character of the crew. Indeed, much of our communicating depends on the transmission of only basic information. We have the capacity to transmit much more than the elementary "one if by land and two if by sea" type of message, but we don't use it. We settle for few data in most of our contacts with others because we would be socially and psychologically demolished if we offered more information about ourselves and, in response, were treated as though we did not exist.

The next time someone asks how you are, tell him! Tell him what ailments you have been having all winter—or tell him you have a hangover, your head is about to split wide open, and you wonder why you ever came to work. Then see what happens. More than likely, you will elicit a nervous laugh or an uncomfortable, "I've got to be on my way," which reflects your listener's complete unreadiness to receive any detailed information on the state of your health.

## The Bare Minimum

The purpose of ritualized communication, then, is usually clear; it is a form of recognizing the speaker's role or defining the role of the listener. In henyard fashion, it is a simple means of defining the "pecking order." We should not, however, deprecate this process of giving each other the recognition we crave and need; one of the most important yearnings of man is for recognition. The single most devastating thing one person can do to another—more devastating than striking out at him with the purpose of injury—is to ignore him altogether. When parents attend only to the physical needs of a child, the usual result is emotional incompetence (psychotic state, schizophrenia, or the like) even before he is old enough to enter school.

Eric Berne, the author of *Games People Play*, calls the process of exchanging meaningless amenities "stroking activity." Intended only to recognize someone, it is nevertheless a form of communication that is both necessary and fulfilling. Without it, people tend to shrivel up and become psychologically and socially incompetent. To prove this, if you want further evidence, deliberately use the technique of non-communication and observe its results. Say nothing to someone—say, an employee—for two or three days if you dare. Not only will the experience be shattering for at least one person, but you yourself will also find it uncomfortable and your behavior will spawn the direst of rumors. Be ready to duck, too, if the person you are ignoring has a hot temper. He will probably reach his boiling point quickly.

Try ignoring your wife and children. Try saying nothing at all to the attendant at the service station where you usually do business. Try staying completely quiet throughout a conference with your co-workers. You will soon be the focus of nervous glances. Their behavior will become erratic and generally upset.

And this test can be extended even further: If someone is inciting others to dislike or distrust you, the most effective way to handle him is to be completely open and communicative with everyone—including him. The surest way to get people to take sides with him against you is to get angry and start threatening him. People then will begin to wonder if there isn't some substance in what he says, for human beings almost instinctively ascribe some measure of truth to any statement that provokes too violent a reaction. Hence the speed with which rumors spread.

If you happen to be a celebrity, ignoring people probably won't make a lot of difference one way or the other; there will be rumors about you whatever you say and do. But you can kill those rumors quickly if you will just ignore them. People will think they cannot be true. Direct attack, criticism, or belittling produces a predictably defensive reaction. Most people are prepared to deal with criticism and the ordinary insults resulting from interpersonal conflict; they fight back. In fact, in the absence of affection and tenderness between parents and children or between husbands and wives, the next best thing is the stimulation of a good squabble. The least acceptable state of affairs is total silence. It is intolerable because it is totally ambiguous—which is why, to repeat, in daily communication we suffer a good deal of strictly ritualized noise, with no real information transmitted.

## Ritual Not Enough

Ritualized communication, to be sure, does more than merely impart information about willingness to extend recognition: It also communicates the degree of our pleasure or displeasure at doing so. Any signal at all says you recognize the other person, without defining the quality of that recognition. But one signal can reflect pleasure and two signals displeasure. Two bits of information are transmitted: "I recognize you," and, "My recognition of you is pleasurable or not pleasurable."

This is a parsimonious process, to say the least, and we may decry its lack of richness. In day-to-day affairs, however, ritualized communication identifies the fundamental poles of personal feeling and provides at least the essentials through which people can get along with one another in a complex society. That is, it provides the minimum "strokes" that people seem to need in order to maintain their psychological health and have some rudimentary sense of where they stand with others.

At the same time, though ritualized communication serves some very important purposes, it is not enough. To get to know another person at all well, and to learn his concerns, needs, drives, and goals, considerably more information has to be transmitted. The trouble is that, particularly in a business setting, the first attempts to move from ritual to the full richness of communication are often distressing to all concerned. Heretofore, each has spoken from behind a protective façade of conventional phrases which keeps everyone from becoming involved with anyone else. It is nearly impossible, for example, to get a long-time employee to open up to the boss and say what he really thinks and feels. It may, indeed, be intolerable for both boss and employee. Yet, to discover one another—to find out what makes one another "tick," in colloquial usage—this must go beyond superficialities.

Essentially, therefore, ritualized communication should be viewed as far more than a convenient means of meeting the basic need for recognition and contact between people. It should help remind people of the opportunity to communicate in real depth if necessary, and it should be seen as providing a barrier or test of the willingness of people to achieve that greater depth of communication.

## Line of Defense

If, in response to a friendly, "Good morning! How are you?" someone says, "Just fine *today!*" he may be suggesting that he did not feel fine yesterday. Such a variation in message may be a subtle cue that a response would be welcome. "Oh? Have you been ill?" But few people will respond without confirmation of such a hint that the speaker may have been ill. To follow the rule of two, if two cues indicate that this interpretation is correct, then it will be logical to ask the follow-up question.

The point is that ritualized communication is often loaded with subtle cues which, combined with other available information, suggest areas that may be worth exploring. Many people have a strong desire for something more than just the superficial amenities of social contact, and they build hints into their responses to reflect this desire. We need only be receptive—and herein lies one purpose of all ritual: It is a way of preserving the opportunities for further contact until someone is willing to respond to them. It forms a line of defense for the individual by protecting him from a harsh and complex world. Ritualized communication continually reminds us that we can get to know other people better. Yet, in its superficiality, it is also a barrier because it satisfies our basic communicative needs.

It is not easy to go beyond ritualized communication. For one thing, it lulls us too readily into being satisfied with minimum gratification of our need for social contacts. We accept the sure, small payoff in preference to the chancy but larger one that might be obtained from communicating in greater depth. In the end, our very senses are dulled; we no longer hear much of what is said to us. Or perhaps it would be more correct to say that we screen out everything extraneous to the basic ritual because we do not expect or want to hear anything else. In the process we become so habituated to basic messages only ("I see you"/"I like you") that we lose the ability to use information beyond this level.

The fact that ritualized communication is a line of defense which protects our self-esteem and our ego becomes, in short, a compelling reason for hearing only what we choose to hear. By attending to only the essentials, we keep out some of the more distressing, negative, self-deprecatory information. In a heated argument, for example, our most pressing motivation is to get our own points across; we are so busy planning our next clever remark or thinking up justifications for our point of view that we do not listen to the other person's point of view. Many people never learn how to listen; they never develop receptiveness because they have never needed or wanted to hear what anyone else had to say.

The art of putting aside one's own fears, desires, and needs so as to give full attention to the needs, concerns, and fears of others is a sophisticated skill which few people ever master, yet a wealth of information and understanding is available to the individual who develops this skill and uses it. The manager, in particular, must quickly pick up cues and follow them through to determine the real concerns and needs of his subordinates and associates and thus know the subjective realities of the organization in which he operates. It might even be appropriate for most companies to require explicitly that their managers learn to listen. Many corporate problems could be solved or at least lessened if such a skill were a prerequisite for managerial appointment.

We should not, of course, overlook the fact that numerous people ignore the simple cues they receive—perhaps because they have neither time nor energy to track them down. In such cases, the chance to communicate may simply be deferred till later. But it may be that the listener finds the implications of the cue disturbing and therefore does not choose to recognize it. For instance, when an employee lets his boss know that he feels his salary is inadequate, it may be best for the manager not to respond to the signal until he has investigated for himself whether the employee's salary is right and, if necessary, has made arrangements for a raise. The cues accompanying ritualized communication, in other words, need not be followed up immediately and discussed fully. It is perhaps enough that the message be perceived and taken into account in the future activities of the hearer.

Receptiveness does not necessarily require responsiveness. It does, however, require a willingness and an ability to perceive what is going on.

## The Smoke Screen

Much ritualized communication is indeed a cover for discussions which the individual is unwilling or perhaps afraid to bring out into the open. The employee who regularly complains that his salary is inadequate may, in reality, be concerned about something else. The true issue may be that he despises his job and feels he should be paid more for doing such undesirable work or that, even though he enjoys his assignment, he feels it offers little opportunity for advancement to a higher position. In the latter case, concern about salary is a smoke screen for concern about advancement.

It used to be that anyone who really wanted to cut some celebrity down to size would obtain a book, a speech, or an article he had written and do a grammatical analysis of it. Making a mistake in English was considered tantamount to admitting to a complete lack of general intelligence. Woodrow Wilson, for example, was once criticized for making "nine grammatical errors in a single sentence." Indeed, an entire book was written in an attempt to prove President Wilson's inability to use the English language correctly.

In our time, with the written language debased in many quarters, a popular way of denigrating someone is to criticize his skill as a public speaker. The great popularity of courses which build public-speaking ability and self-confidence attests to the anxiety of many people about being able to "speak on their feet." It is tacitly accepted that the man who freezes when he gets up to speak has little claim to competence.

Both "proper" English and "correct" public-speaking techniques are really only ritualized efforts to teach ritualized communication so that people may speak and write acceptably, without fear of criticism. If you obey all the rules, it is suggested, you cannot get into trouble. But ritualized communication practiced to a fine degree remains ritual, and it is an unnecessarily limited means of exchanging information. In contrast, there are few if any courses on "how to make yourself understood." It is probably just as well—if such courses existed, they would be particularly difficult to teach and they would probably not be at all popular. Making yourself understood is no simple matter. Often, the reward for attempting to be understood is to be misunderstood, and the reward for being misunderstood is to be disliked.

When we try for something more than the most elementary communication, however, the risk of being misunderstood or even disliked must be taken. If we are interested in communicating fully, it is not enough to become polished in our speech or writing. The real point is not polish, but substance. The essence of many a highly polished communication is one message: The speaker adores himself.

## Ability to Communicate = Ability to Explore

Communication between human beings is, at best, a crude process. As compared to attempts to communicate with a computer, it is incredibly sloppy and imprecise. The precision of mathematics pervades the entire effort to communicate with modern, automated equipment; whereas, with people, we assume that precision is not so necessary. Our day-to-day communication with one another is therefore redundant and inefficient.

What is surprising is that so many of our efforts are accurately perceived. In ordinary conversation we seldom use an exact or even a complete sentence. We string words and phrases together, and inflections and gurgles to punctuate them, and hope for the best. We rely heavily on convention and the latest jargon and fad words. And we add language which is thought of as "dirty" to shock or capture the full attention of the listener (even ritualizing the shock process in our communication).

If we really want to get a message across, as any practitioner of the art will advise us, we are obliged to repeat it over and over again. We stick to a single theme and say it in as many ways as we can in the hope that somehow the message will get across. As we move out of the realm of ritualized noise, we begin to use not just one or two messages but hundreds and even thousands of them.

Repetition, in short, is our basic means of insuring the reliability of communication. As listeners, we examine each incoming message and compare it with the last to see how it fits. Out of a series of messages we put together a mental image of the idea being conveyed.

Carefully arranged and juxtaposed repetition is, as is well known, the method used in programmed instruction. Research on programmed texts indicates that they tend to have a flatness and dullness that is not characteristic of ordinary, and hence more literary, texts on the same subjects. The result is that almost everyone taught by a programmed text achieves the same moderate level of proficiency, whereas students who learn from a standard text differ more widely in the degree of skill they acquire. Apparently the unsystematic process of communication which goes into the typical textbook for school or business use provides salient insights for some students while, for others, it creates confusion which prevents or inhibits learning.

There are distinct rewards and distinct pitfalls to be found when we go beyond ritualized communication. There is much greater room for confusion and misunderstanding than would be likely if our communication were as precise as the mathematical formulations designed for input to a computer. On the other hand, there is also an opportunity to leave mere words, phrases, and sentences behind and communicate a much greater depth and breadth of ideas.

Human communication offers, in fact, a chance to explore the fullest range of human capability. It opens the outer frontiers of the world and permits us to read more than is actually in the printed word and hear more than is actually said. The richness inherent in such communication is worth seeking for its own sake.

## Performance Versus Communication

Frequently, as we have already implied, our problem in ritualized communication is that we are too busy performing. For example, consider the quality of communication which occurs when an actor delivers set lines and goes through prescribed motions. He may communicate with us as a person in some very special ways, apparently achieving a depth of understanding and skill in portrayal that is noteworthy. But, as for the content of his message, he is merely a medium of communication for the author and the director of the play.

Similarly, the employee who carries out his manager's instructions with great care and effectiveness may be expressing his willingness to participate in the work of the organization and be a competent member of the group, but he is communicating nothing more than his ability to carry out his prescribed function. He is a medium which the manager merely uses for getting results.

Too often, we are confused into accepting performance as an act of communication on the part of the performer. This confusion is perhaps natural in connection with stage plays or movies because, in such situations, we may find it impossible to determine who is really trying to communicate with us, but it is essential that the words which pass between people in everyday life not to be construed to mean more than they do.

When the company president stops at an employee's work station to ask how he likes his work, the employee is performing the role expected of him when he expresses enjoyment and appreciation of his work. More likely than not, however, the only real message being communicated by this performance is an appreciation for the manager's concern with the employee's feelings about his work. And even this message of appreciation may be left out of the employee's response if he senses that the manager also is performing and that the question is perfunctory.

We are inclined to accept as the literal and final truth Shakespeare's description of the world as a stage and the people in it as players. This view of life, unfortunately, leaves no room for creative, innovative, or unique problem solving. Performance is an acceptable substitute for communication as long as there are no problems to be solved. When demonstrated ability in standardized tasks and behavior is all that is needed, performance will suffice. But when established standards and ready-made solutions will *not* do, performance gets in the way.

## How to Discriminate

It is worthwhile, therefore, to learn to discriminate between performance and communication. The mark of performance is that it typically—

- ✧ Follows a prescribed pattern.
- ✧ Involves competition with others in which excellence is sought.
- ✧ Cannot tolerate variations in the pattern and even sees such variations as failure.
- ✧ Defines the conclusion of the effort as the achievement of the traditional or accepted pattern of behavior.

In other words, performance in this sense is a mechanical act which is learned through practice and repetition.

The signs of communication, on the other hand, are very different and in many respects quite the opposite:

- ✧ The unique needs of each participant are carefully explored, and one's communicative efforts are adapted to them.
- ✧ There is no competition and no win/lose relationship; that is, one person does not gain at the expense of the other. If communication is successful, both parties gain.
- ✧ Errors are accepted as inevitable and, indeed, necessary; they are seen as evidence of a sincere effort to develop genuine understanding.
- ✧ The conclusion of the effort comes only when understanding is achieved. This means there may never be a conclusion in situations where understanding is never fully achieved. (In the realm of communication, it is safe to assume that total understanding between two people is impossible and

that the best that can be hoped for is partial understanding
in certain areas—achieved through sincere and arduous effort by both parties.)

The identifying signs of communication clearly include a lack of
planning and control over what is done. Communication requires
openness, randomness, trial and error, and exploration of previously
untried paths. It does not follow the beaten path; it goes where the
participants are and focuses on their needs and experiences. Above all,
it makes no simplistic, mechanical assumptions about the communication process itself.

Against these criteria, most communication carried on in areas like
business—whether it be internal communication among managers and
employees or external communication, such as advertising, directed
toward others—is more accurately described as performance. Perhaps
the real expert on Madison Avenue in recent years has been the individual who, within the framework of the restraints placed upon him
by the rituals of advertising, could find ways to communicate meaningfully with people through the medium of advertising. It doesn't
happen often; and, when it does, it is quickly noticed.

## Choice of Styles

For our everyday communication we may choose one or a combination of three distinct styles. First, we may rely on conventional,
highly ritualized performance which reliably transmits a limited
amount of information. We may tip our hat and say, "Good morning," to the secretary down the hall as a way of acknowledging her
presence. We may make sounds indicative of unhappiness to show
our displeasure of some event. We may exclaim, "No, that's not what
I mean at all!" when we detect an error in the recipient's understanding of our message. We may shake hands, smile, hold a door
open, wave to someone in a car, or use literally thousands of other
conventional gestures and words in communicating with people. This
is a limited way of using our communicative potential; but it is,
nevertheless, a reliable and necessary way.

Second, we may try to attain more precision by defining phrases,
terms, or ideas as carefully as possible to insure full understanding.

This is the style of the computer program. Its principal deficiency lies in its inability to cope with so much as a single error which may invalidate the entire effort. It can, however, be very effective in eliminating a certain amount of confusion in our communication with people.

Third, we may attempt with words, gestures, and expressions of every sort to communicate more deeply with others. We may use words in a literary way to express our emotions and our most complex ideas. We may rely heavily on reiteration as a way of seeking understanding.

If we choose the second or third of these alternatives, we will complicate our communicative efforts considerably. Errors will be introduced by the hundreds. Because of these errors, we can never be satisfied with one-way communication; we must develop means of closing the loop so that our messages are transmitted back to us and we can detect and correct any misperceptions, misunderstandings, or simple errors due to noise in the channel. It will no longer be enough to exhort; we must somehow arrange a dialogue.

For the manager, this is easier said than done. His position as a judge of performance puts the employee perpetually on the defensive and makes it very difficult—if not impossible—to obtain open, candid feedback as to the employee's perceptions of the manager's inputs. The manager's position as a competitor, along with his fellow managers, for promotion and rewards within the organization also makes it hard for him to establish candid, open communication with his peers. Finally, his subordinate status vis-à-vis higher levels of management may put him in a position where open, unfettered communication is perceived as difficult or even dangerous. The safest communication for him will always be conventional and ritualized.

When this will not suffice to solve his problems, what does the manager do? The pages that follow will attempt to answer this question. In Part Two, types of communication will be surveyed which can be used in face-to-face contacts between a superior and his subordinate. Then, in Part Three, the act of affecting meaningful communication between the individual and the organization will be explored.

# 5

————— ◆•◆ —————

## *The Technology*
## *of Communication*

IT WOULD BE a gross understatement to say that improvements in technology in recent years have had a marked effect on communication. It has been suggested, for example, that the one factor most responsible for encouraging a new feeling of nationalism among the Arabs in the Middle East in recent years has been the transistor radio. No longer does it make any difference whether the individual Arab is in the city market place or in a desert oasis; his radio keeps him up to date and immediately involved in the events of the day.

To the extent that the reporting of those events presents the Arab point of view, the individual town or oasis dweller is being influenced to accept its nationalistic interpretation of world affairs. From our rather lofty and "unbiased" viewpoint, we would call it propaganda; in the Middle East, it is merely truth as seen through Arab eyes. Without the transistor no such "truth" would be known in the Arab world; the individual "Arab in the street" would still be dependent on word-of-mouth communication or, if he is literate, on some sort of written or published information. With the transistor, however, he need only be able to understand his own language to know what is going on throughout the vast reaches of his universe. Thus his emotions and actions can easily and reliably be directed to the objectives of nationalism.

Perhaps the impact of radio on the Arabs should have come as less of a surprise to us. Americans, both children and adults, are only a little less inclined to accept uncritically what they hear on radio or see on television. After all, as Westerners who have been familiar with rapid communication through the media of radio and television for most of our lives, we are well aware of the impact which once remote and mysterious occurrences may now have. Television, for instance, makes it possible for us to observe many events which, in earlier days, we would have learned about only through the stories of others. The sinking of the battleship Maine in Havana harbor and the charge of Teddy Roosevelt and his Rough Riders up San Juan Hill during the Spanish-American War might have been much less romanticized if television cameras had been on the scene to record them in all their stark reality, and the American public would probably have received a much more factual version of what happened.

In contrast with the days of San Juan Hill, the civilian populations of the world have come to experience a kind of involvement in the Vietnam war, unlike anything ever known before, as a result of the intensive reporting which television permits. Because of television, too, the individual citizen can be "present" at important events— conferences of world leaders, debates between nations, coronations, and national tragedies—with only a minimum of interruption by an interpreter. A century ago such events could have been covered solely by word of mouth and written correspondence.

One curious consequence of these advances in technology is that there is less standardization of opinion about what is happening than there may once have been. Before the advent of electronic telecommunications, one interpretation of a nationally or internationally important event was likely to prevail. True, there were different versions depending upon what newspaper or magazine you read (each gave you its particular point of view); and if you could obtain a second publication, you probably were exposed to one more interpretation. Still, by and large, people tended to accept the first available interpretation, so that the story published first was likely to set the tone of opinion.

This, however, is no longer the case. The publication of a news story becomes more and more of an anticlimax to the event itself. The more direct the observation of the actual event, the greater the potential diversity of interpretation. Individuals can discuss an incident and discover innumerable differences of perspective in what they saw. Thus a speech by the President of the United States is interpreted by one person as an indication that things are improving and by another as proof that disaster is right around the corner.

Our technological aids to communication have complicated life immeasurably. Events are having a greater and greater effect on our lives, and we can no longer ignore them. Instead, we are often forced to realize how complex they are, and more and more often we are confused or frustrated by our lack of a clear understanding of them. This is not a new problem, of course; it has always existed for the literate and well read. Access to multiple sources of information about important events has always made interested men and women aware of the complexities of life and the resulting problems of communication.

There have always been those, naturally, who were ready to decry as foolish any inclination to wonder about events. "Anybody with a little common sense can see what it's all about" has been their reaction to efforts to understand and interpret major changes in the environment. Unfortunately, however, this common-sense approach may be little more than a folksy way of trying to coax others into accepting one's own point of view. Information and communication are complicated and difficult matters; to treat them as anything less is to delude ourselves. The development of commercial television, closed-circuit television, automated typesetting, instant photography, and all the other marvels of our time can be immensely useful in improving our ability to become and remain well informed. But they also point up the real problems of understanding the world we live in and of communicating effectively with our fellow man.

## More Information, Less Time

We must not treat lightly the impact on effective communication of increased efficiency in the reproduction and publication of written matter. Far more printed information is available than ever before. Modern copying devices make it possible quickly and cheaply to inform limitless numbers of people about our activities and interests or about events we have witnessed.

This increased ability to publish has two effects, one positive and one negative. The positive effect is that needed information can get to those people best able to solve the problems of business, government, and society. On the negative side, the average businessman's in-basket and the typical homeowner's mailbox are now filled with incredible quantities of material. Some people are close to being overwhelmed by the amount of reading matter confronting them every day. Courses and books on how to increase reading speed have zoomed to unprecedented popularity. It is now as common for managers to delegate the reading and evaluation of reports and of job-related publications as it is to delegate any other kind of work.

In like fashion, improved, lower-cost telephone and wire service also has increased the amount of time people devote to the communication of information. Business managers have always spent a good part of their time in meetings at which information and points of view are shared. Now they seem to spend almost all their time in meetings, on the telephone, or in reading.

But the problem goes beyond just reading, listening, and discussion. We now have more information than we can use or synthesize adequately in the time available. Businessmen, in particular, need better summaries of data. Some of the most important new business functions are those concerned with obtaining, interpreting, and processing information for dissemination to higher management. The technical breakthrough in this area has been made in recent decades by the computer, which is capable of handling enormous quantities of information; when existing methods for summarizing and reporting information are not adequate, a computer can be put to excellent use in preparing facts and figures for use by management. However, much remains to be done. Methods of summarizing highly complex and often contradictory information must be improved, the computer must become as much a personal tool of the individual manager in solving data-reduction problems as the automobile is a personal tool in solving transportation problems.

Indeed, the computer's potential for effecting changes in the methods of managing a business or even of running a household is substantial. This potential has been obscured by the predictions of many computer technologists, scientists, and businessmen as to what the computer can do. The common belief that it is comparable to the human brain bespeaks the incredible expectations many people have of it. In reality, though, the computer is nothing more than a machine whose usefulness is based on its capacity to process small bits of information in tremendous quantities. Everything fed into a computer, whether it be letters of the alphabet or other symbols, must first be reduced to codes which can be stored as bits. If the information is too theoretical or too unreal to be reduced to that form, the computer cannot process it. What we think of as incredible performance is nothing more than the swift manipulation of untold millions of bits of information.

The computer accepts what is fed into it uncritically and processes this input into a predictable output. For, given full knowledge of what is going into the machine, it is entirely possible to say exactly what will result. In this ability to predict, indeed, lies the great utility of the computer: It will carry out orders better than the fastest, most efficient person can. It will fail only when the equipment suffers a physical breakdown or when it is given instructions that are ambiguous or meaningless. In this sense the computer is like any other tool that man has developed—automobile, lathe, airplane, typewriter, can opener, or whatever. That is, it performs specific, well-defined functions far more efficiently and at far lower cost than they could be performed manually. This is the true role for the computer in the future—to free human time and energy for the solution of human problems.

The *best* way to solve any problem is always to turn it over to a fully competent human being who is challenged by it, who is experienced with the elements involved, and who finds satisfaction in seeking a solution to it. Let him process the available information through his brain and try out a variety of alternatives until he arrives at the best solution within the constraints of time and material resources. Thus, when you want a manufacturing operation run effectively, you put in charge of it an experienced man who is interested in it, and you give him responsibility for figuring out what is going on and for making the necessary decisions. In the same way, when you want a great city run well, you look for someone experienced or trained in the handling of municipal problems and let him wade into the mass of pertinent data until he understands the situation thoroughly and can come up with a series of artful solutions.

Our dilemma in this age is that the amount of information that must be digested and summarized in order to solve the problems of businesses, cities, and nations is so great that it is rapidly exceeding the capacity of any one human being to deal with it. There was a time when a dispute between a city government and the employees of a municipal service such as public transportation could be settled by means of a wage increase and some concessions in working conditions. Nowadays the tremendous inconveniences that are caused by a transit strike, the impact of the settlement on the city's total economic structure, the trade-offs that have to be considered relative to other transportation systems or labor groups, and many other fantastically complex considerations have to be brought into play in order to arrive at a solution that is sensible and fully acceptable in terms of the future. And the future arrives fast; any mortgages we take out on it—in the way of deferred problems—will be back at our doorstep to plague us all too soon. It is in connection with just such a situation that the computer can realize its fullest potential as an adjunct to human ability.

## The Trouble with the Computer

One fundamental difficulty with the computer in its present stage of development lies in this fact: Few people other than data processing experts know how to make use of it as a personal tool; most people need an interpreter to help them with it.

An analogy may be drawn between the computer and the automobile. In the early days, when motor vehicles were temperamental and unreliable, someone who could fix them had to be on hand at all times; the man at the wheel therefore had to be an expert mechanic as well as an expert driver. In those days few people learned to be either. Nowadays, in contrast, reliability and simplicity of operation have made the automobile a personal tool of much of the population, allowing an individual to satisfy his own needs for transportation and mobility.

The computer is now in a stage of development comparable to the early days of the automobile. When the average manager wants to make use of the computer, he must go to a systems man, explain his needs, hope he is understood, wait while the systems man explains the problem to the computer programmer, hope that nothing is lost in the various translations, wait some more while the programmer tells a machine operator what to do with the program, and, finally, view the output of all this effort in the form of processed information. By this time, typically, the amount of money invested in designing a system, programming it, and putting it on the computer is so high that only managers with very liberal budgets and excellent profit positions can afford it.

Using the computer under these conditions is comparable to riding in a chauffeured limousine. To make the computer the kind of readily available personal tool the automobile is today requires that the real user of the computer—that is, the manager or technical specialist—be put into the driver's seat as rapidly as possible. In other words, ways must be found to permit people with information-processing problems to use the computer directly in solving those problems much as they would use a shovel, an automobile, or a typewriter to solve quite different problems.

The computer, however, is so complex a tool that there will always have to be some kind of mediating arrangement. The fact is that a single problem may reduce to millions of separate pieces of information. The manager who is working on it cannot be expected to concern himself with every one of those pieces in the way required for successful operation of a computer. Certain kinds of standard programs must therefore be developed which will enable the computer user to communicate directly with it in terms of large and comprehensive concepts. When a manager wants the names of a thousand employees arranged alphabetically, he must not be bogged down in the myriad bits of detail required by the computer to effect the output. What he wants to be able to do is to instruct the computer: "Alphabetize the names of my employees and give me a list of them."

Fortunately, functions like these are gradually being standardized, and a wide variety of common information-handling needs are being met. It is feasible now to regard the computer as an incredibly efficient tool for handling information in vast quantities far more rapidly, effectively, and cheaply than any human clerk could be expected to handle it. These "software" developments, as they are called in the industry, are occurring much more slowly than many people would like. But they are, nevertheless, coming about; and, as they are more and more generally available, the computer can be used in increasing numbers by managers, employees, students, teachers, and anyone else who has an information-processing problem.

However, in those instances where the computer has been successfully put to immediate personal use by people other than data processing experts, a new problem has begun to emerge—the problem of how to interpret and summarize data. It is one thing to handle 562 items of information on 44,000 product lines in a corporation, but it is something else again to find meaningful, consistent interrelationships in that information which will permit dealing with large chunks of it at one time.

In the past, management decisions have been made largely "by the seat of the pants." The manager put himself into the middle of the problem, became intimately familiar with all its aspects and ramifications, and made his decision on the basis of his emotional reaction as much as any other. That is, he solved much of his problem artfully rather than systematically. At times, however, something more logical is required, and the process of developing the right kind of logic is no simple matter.

This is where the computer enters in. While—to repeat—the most satisfying way to solve almost any problem is to let one highly competent human being become intimately familiar with it and work out a solution to it on the basis of his feeling for it, converting this approach into logical procedures is a vitally necessary but extremely difficult task which is the real challenge for the future so far as EDP is concerned. It is a challenge because we cannot decide to inject ourselves into a nuclear holocaust on the basis of anything less than the full facts about any threat to our national security. It is a challenge because, when a surgeon transplants human organs from one body to another, he must have all the relevant information immediately available in order to make the right decisions as he operates. It is a challenge because, as cities strangle in garbage and struggle with air pollution, social disorganization, and near-anarchy in the streets, we cannot depend solely upon the artful "feel" of some politician's pronouncement that may decide the fate of millions. It is a challenge because, in sending a man to the moon, we cannot merely hope that the people involved in the project will have considered all the problems that must be dealt with prior to the making of critical decisions.

The computer is already being used to solve many of these problems: for instance, to check out all the components of the rocket boosters, the spacecraft, and related systems in the current space program. Its use here is absolutely essential. Without the computer to handle the tremendous flow of information that must be processed and acted upon, it would not be possible to launch a man into orbit around the earth or plot a course intended to land him on the moon.

Despite all this, however, the processes by which information is summarized are still desperately inadequate, particularly with respect to the major social problems of our age. Throughout history, social problems have been left to philosophers, mystics, and theologians. Today, in contrast, the people who have the real power and economic resources, and whose contribution to the solution of major social problems is vital and critical, must move into this realm and begin to make order out of haphazard procedures. This will be a strange new venture for men of practical bent who are oriented toward results.

## Compensating for Human Limitations

The typical human being is habituated to dealing with only two, three, four, or at most five variants in his environment at one time. Most decisions about people—that is, most stereotypes about them—are based on such factors as last name, sex, manner of dress, manner of speech, and physical appearance. These are used to make judgments as to a person's character—and, to some degree, this process is successful. Stereotypes are perhaps better than random guesses about other people. Nevertheless, they are highly inadequate and too often wrong. This is precisely the kind of information-processing problem to which the computer may one day be applied.

By permitting the average person to overcome the gross deficiencies in his information-processing capabilities, the computer will enable him to make much sounder, more accurate predictions about people. The result will be fewer errors about human beings and fewer misunderstandings among them. Until we reach this point—in other words, until dozens or even hundreds of separate, distinct items of information about one individual can be processed to come up with a highly reliable forecast of his abilities and behavior—we will not progress beyond our present state of civilization and human capacity!

Make no mistakes about it: The change effected by computers in the quality of life and in our approach to problem solving will be dramatic. It will be no less dramatic, however, than the difference between traveling across the United States in a covered wagon and flying across it in a jet plane. Anyone who still wants to travel by covered wagon in an attempt to recapture the life of his forebears may do so. But there can be no denying the fact that the quality of human relationships has changed vastly because of the shift in the means of travel across the country, and something akin to this degree of change can be anticipated as the computer becomes a more commonly used personal tool.

The obvious need for this more effective tool—that is, a better information-processing system—in solving the problems of mankind cannot be overstated. Our salvation may indeed lie in our ability to adapt the technology quickly to the full range of our needs. In order to do this, however, we must sweep aside the concept of a computer as a mystical instrument which only the anointed few are able to comprehend and use. We must see it for what it is—a machine which, in many respects, is less complicated than an automobile.

The task we face as individuals in attempting to master the computer and use it in day-to-day problem solving is the task of learning how to communicate with it effectively. One of the first things we must learn is that the computer seldom makes errors, while the human operator makes them frequently. This can be a crushing blow to the human ego, but there is more to come: We soon discover that many of our instructions are so poorly thought out, badly phrased, ambiguous, irrational, or incomprehensible that we cannot get any utility out of the computer at all.

The truth of the matter is that the computer will not make up for deficiencies in our communication skills unless we have anticipated these deficiencies and told the computer how to deal with them. Every problem fed to the machine must be worked out step by step in precise, logical form, without so much as one error in the position of a comma, period, or other symbol. The entire effort can fail because of one trivial mistake. The discipline this calls for frequently startles people who never before have been required to communicate so precisely. It can be terrifying to realize that virtually every communication we pass along to others contains errors or ambiguities that may cause total misunderstanding; that, in fact, much of the information we have been transmitting and receiving is misunderstood and our assumptions about the accuracy of our communications are no longer acceptable.

Learning to live with the computer, in short, will probably be one of the most startling and important experiences that anyone who fancies himself a communicator is ever likely to undergo. Far from having misgivings about this state of affairs, however, he should welcome it. For the first time, he—and many people with him—will be forced to face the fact that he doesn't know what he is saying. Such a realization may go further toward solving basic human problems in this world than any other single factor.

Over all, then, we can expect that the impact of the computer will be dramatic, although we cannot predict the direction of the qualitative changes in life and in communication that will result. One thing, nevertheless, we can be sure of: Our problems will not begin to yield to solution until the computer's real potential is quickly and fully exploited by every man of practical affairs, be he manager, politician, or technician. Only then will the computer become as important in solving today's urgent social problems as agricultural machinery has proved in eliminating famine and hunger.

## The Audiovisual Element

It is hardly necessary to describe in detail the advances in audiovisual communication techniques which have occurred in recent years.

Take the almost hyperdramatic impact of Cinerama. Its massive field of view nearly approximates the limits of our peripheral vision, and its stereophonic sound loads our ears with all the aural sensations we can tolerate. This new medium alone attests to the efficiency with which we can put across a story audiovisually.

Moreover, it is technically possible to overload the senses even with the movies now being produced and shown in ordinary movie houses. Recent experiments with multiple 35-millimeter slides projected onto multiple screens in much the same fashion as Cinerama demonstrate that an impelling visual and aural impact can be obtained from equipment as basic as a set of three slide projectors and a tape recorder. Work is now under way at the University of Southern California on the development of a simple control device which would coordinate the simultaneous use of three 35-millimeter projectors, one or more film projectors, and a synchronized tape recorder. The advantages are low cost and high flexibility. An impressive audiovisual presentation can be offered on a low budget, and material can be revised or updated almost at will, by using this combination of simple and inexpensive equipment.

And, even as such innovations are being developed, rapid advances in television technology—including inexpensive closed-circuit equipment and tape recorders for the preservation and playback of film— are pointing the way to the future. The day may soon come when every business will have a presentation room in which a screen that nearly surrounds the viewer and a high-fidelity stereophonic sound system will be used to process, orient, and train new employees; to present courses to managers throughout the company's many locations; to brief visitors or customers on the company's products; or to make progress reports to board members or stockholders.

Technological advances make it easier to employ the best talents and the best ideas in order to create as forceful and effective a communication presentation as possible for any audience, large or small. At the same time, the onward race of technology is increasing the number of people who are able to make up their own minds and insist upon their right to do so; more, better, and less expensive methods of communicating have helped put an increasing number of people into direct touch with the important events of our times. Increasingly, too, these people are unwilling to settle for talk and are insistent upon effective action. If this is, in fact, one outcome of improved communications technology, we can look to the future with considerable confidence.

It may be true that advances in communications technology have complicated the world for some people in ways we could never have dreamed of. Many of the mental and physical breakdowns characteristic of our age undoubtedly stem from the overwhelming complexity and attendant confusion which modern technology has brought to life. We have exceeded the limits of human capability in at least some instances, thus creating new problems to be solved.

But, as more and more people become capable of interpreting the facts for themselves, there should be fewer opportunities for charlatans, con artists, or demagogues to sway the masses of the world to their own purposes. It will be to the credit of the communications-technology explosion that it has created a generation of men and women who can and do think for themselves.

# PART TWO

*Man/Manager Communication*

# 6

*The Broadcast Model*

*of Communication*

ALMOST INEVITABLY, three problems affect the communication climate in any business setting:

1. Employees frequently believe it is safer *not* to communicate.
2. Because of the hierarchical nature of organizations, upward communication can be summarily shut off by the next-higher level of management.
3. The person in authority can readily assume that it is his subordinate's responsibility to communicate effectively with him, rather than his to communicate effectively with the subordinate.

Let us look at each of these problems in detail.

*Penalties and rewards.* Organizations frequently exact costly penalties from the individual who fails to make himself understood. A member of the company who sends a message that cannot be interpreted correctly by its receivers is likely to be held personally accountable for any ensuing problems and to be punished for having been ineffective in his efforts to communicate. This state of affairs—which is by no means unique to business organizations—often results in a tendency to avoid becoming involved. The person who displays this tendency has learned that the penalties of being misunderstood are so much greater than the rewards of having been understood that involvement is not worth the risk.

Consider the case of an employee who becomes aware that instructions from higher management have been erroneously transmitted. For example, the general manager's secretary is told by her boss, "This order must be shipped by the manufacturing department no later than June 21st." She then forwards a directive which reads "July 21st." An administrative assistant in the same office sees the directive and suspects that a mistake has been made in the date. He calculates the consequences of attempting to straighten out the mistake and decides that the secretary might be very angry at anyone who questioned her accuracy. She might even begin to look for errors on *his* part if he were to point out *hers*. His motives could be interpreted as ambitious and self-seeking, and she might be led to believe that he was out to make his own reputation at her expense. If, on the other hand, *he* is in error about the date, he will likely be considered a fool for having questioned it to begin with.

Things will probably be in a real mess if the people in manufacturing attempt to meet the July target date when the general manager expects them to be performing against the June date. However, they have their instructions in writing; if they fail to meet the June date, they can defend themselves by producing the directive and showing that the error was not theirs. This will be accepted as a normal and necessary defense of their position while under attack, whereas the interference of the administrative assistant might be misinterpreted. If our administrative assistant is the practical, experienced, and mildly cynical kind of fellow who realizes the hazards he faces and knows there are no rewards, but only penalties, for pointing out other people's mistakes, we can predict that he will not try to correct the error in advance.

The problem becomes particularly acute whenever a subordinate tries to communicate upward. Suppose a marketing man makes an effort to explain to the general manager that he is opposed to entering a particular market but that, if an entry is to be made, it should be tackled no later than the end of the current year. The general manager misunderstands this statement; he believes the marketing man is insisting on entering the market by the end of the year. If the company does so, and if its experience in the market is poor, the resulting situation could very well lead to the marketing man's dismissal. In this case, the penalty for being misunderstood is very high, while the rewards for being understood are comparatively modest.

The individual who is highly motivated to increase his income or status in the organization may at first be inclined to risk the penalties for being misunderstood. As he observes the penalties paid by others, however, he may decide that it is not worthwhile to communicate when the risk is too high—unless he has no other choice. Much communication, then, may be expected to occur when the manager or employee has his back to the wall and has little choice except to express candidly what needs to be said. But open, timely communication is not common in companies simply because the people in them are fully aware of the truth of the matter: The risks of timely communication are unduly high as compared to the rewards.

*Summary shutoff.* Business organizations are designed to amplify downward communication by exacting severe penalties for failing to hear and heed messages. But the same authority which insures that the manager is heard by his subordinates also grants him the right to refuse to hear them. A manager can summarily reject the upward communication of any or all his employees, should he choose to do so.

In effect, upward communication can be and frequently is shut off or severely muted because of the superior's unwillingness to listen or his readiness to punish people who communicate in ways which displease him. The subordinate who brings to his manager the bad news that they have overreached their budget may well be doing the manager a service by mentioning the trouble before it becomes any more severe, but he may also have to bear the brunt of the manager's ire for being the bearer of bad news. If that is the case, the subordinate will think twice before bringing his boss bad news again, unless he has no other choice.

One method of discipline commonly used in business is to cut the employee off from communication. In other words, the manager freezes the employee out by ignoring any incoming messages while at the same time refusing to transmit any but the most formal, routine work directions. Such situations clearly show the power of the manager, or anyone else in authority, to give or deny the employee a hearing. More commonly, however, communication is cut off quite by accident. An inadvertent reaction by the manager which discourages candid, direct, upward communication by the employee, and which teaches the employee that there is no payoff in attempting it voluntarily, is all too frequent.

*Unwarranted assumptions.* Any person who has authority over another person is in a position to write many of the rules of the relationship as he sees fit. It is easy for the boss to simplify his world by assuming that it is the employee's responsibility to communicate with him and that inability to do so is the employee's tough luck. The boss's reasoning seldom takes so harsh and overt a form; nevertheless, he does, to the detriment of communication, often take the attitude that the communication problem is no concern of his.

The manager who claims to have an open-door policy is often the man who, immediately following a session with an employee, calls the employee's supervisor and asks, "What kind of screwball do you have working for you?" It is situations such as this that place the initiative for communication—and responsibility for its success or failure—in the hands of the employee. If he fails in his efforts to communicate upward, he must bear the consequences for having displeased his manager or for having made a poor impression on higher management.

The rewards for success in upward communication may be very attractive under these conditions. The individual who can make a good impression on higher management may be on his way to advancement. The penalties for failure, however, are usually severe and frequently final.

In these circumstances, upward communication tends to fall into two categories: Either the employee tries but fails and, as a result, must bear a certain stigma for the failure; or second, possessed of more than usual aggressiveness and ability, the employee attempts and succeeds, thereby gaining the attention and perhaps the future favor of higher management. This is not really a system of communication; rather, it is a system of obstacles used to screen and select the most effective communicators for higher-level positions. In the process, upward communication suffers greatly.

## The Basic Method

What then, can management do? In view of the existing barriers, what sort of practical communication system is there which can be used in a business setting between superiors and subordinates? The most typical concept is that of "basic" information transmission, or a "broadcast" model. Within this system there are three elements: the transmitter, the channel (or medium of transmission), and the receiver (see Exhibit 1).

### EXHIBIT 1

### The "Broadcast" Model

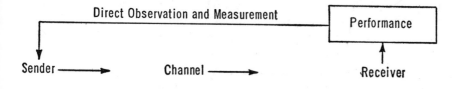

The broadcast model of communication is very useful to the businessman. It is exemplified by radio, television, newspaper, magazines, or direct mail to the customer's home. With this model, the sender decides on the nature of the message he wishes to transmit to his audience, be they customers, stockholders, employees, or anyone else. He next selects his channel of communication, beams out the message, and hopes his audience (the receivers) will get it. He gauges the success of his methods by the types of reactions he gets from his audience. If he is advertising garden seed, he measures his results in terms of increased sales. If sales go up and the extra profits more than cover the cost of advertising, the attempt to communicate is considered successful. Note, however, that the system is one in which only the most basic response to the message is sought.

This is not to deprecate the broadcast method of communicating at all. It can be a useful and profitable way of informing the public of one's wares or services. Indeed, in the early days of broadcasting—before radio or television became so common—people were very receptive to radio messages advising them of available activities, products, and services and acquainting them with the attitude and values of leaders in the community. Even today radio can have considerable impact, and the still greater power of television is so well known as to require little comment. Being able not only to know but to see immediately what is happening a great distance away is an exhilarating experience; furthermore, it conveys a sense of personal participation which encourages an individual, whether housewife, gardener, or teenage pop-music fan, to take full advantage of the opportunities around him—opportunities of which he might be unaware without large-scale broadcast communications.

It is well to keep in mind, however, that the broadcast method should be reserved for direct messages which call for easily observed responses. If we want to sell more garden seed, we can determine our success or failure in communicating with our public; all we need is a cash register in the store to record sales. A road closing, a new cafeteria, a change of rule, a special holiday schedule—all these are grist for broadcasting. The method is effective because errors in perception can be quickly detected and corrected. There is little chance that management will go on believing its employees know the new cafeteria has opened, for example, if they do not use it.

A second important requirement of the broadcast model of communication is simplicity of message content. Any newspaper editor, ad man, or other representative of the mass media knows this. Overcomplexity and technical terminology must be avoided with great care. The manager who wants his employees to know that the new plant cafeteria will be open next week would do well to phrase his message along these straightforward lines:

> The newly installed cafeteria will open for business beginning Monday, January 12, between the hours of 11:30 and 12:45 to serve employees who want to have a hot meal during their lunch hour. The cafeteria is located in the southeast corner of the first floor of Building 1. Access to the cafeteria is through the main entrance or through the south entrance of Building 1.

Contrast this specific and informative message with the following real-life example, taken from an employee magazine:

The management of XY Company is happy to announce that, in response to many requests from employees, hot meals will be made available at lunch time through a complete, new, and modern cafeteria which has been installed on the premises to serve the needs of employees. We believe this is just another in a long series of examples of *enlightened* management decisions which are designed to promote improved management-employee relations and to insure the welfare of our employees.

The first of these two news pieces is designed to provide information important to the employees and elicit a specific response from them. The second is an attempt to convince them of the benevolence of management; it seeks to influence their attitudes toward management—the XY Company hopes that the opening of the cafeteria will win its employees' approval or gratitude and perhaps also help to offset their grievances. Note, however, that the message is complicated and that the behavior being sought is less subject to direct observation and measurement than that invited by the first example. It is, in fact, so loosely related to the news release itself that, even if measurement were attempted, it would be difficult to prove that any behavior change was a direct result of the message.

To compound the problem, many a manager issues a complex message by means of the broadcast model only to discover that the payoff is quite the opposite of what he is trying to achieve. Instead of generating positive feelings toward management, the communication may produce a negative reaction. Thus the new cafeteria, which was intended to demonstrate benevolence in industrial relations, becomes a source of grievances and unending complaints; if anything, employee attitudes are worse. Hard experience has indicated that the broadcast model can be tricky when applied to such a complex matter as effecting a change in attitude, which usually requires a somewhat more sophisticated method of communication.

The broadcast method is recommended for general use in the following circumstances:

1. Whenever highly reliable information is available about the performance of employees, the buying habits of customers, the confidence of stockholders, or the predisposition of government regulatory agencies and the impact of the information can be measured in terms of positive, negative, or neutral response.

2. Whenever the information to be transmitted is simple, straightforward, and subject to a minimum of misunderstanding.
3. Whenever no other method of communicating is feasible because of time, distance, or other constraints.

## Common Techniques

Managers put the basic broadcast method of communication into operation by means of several different techniques (see Exhibit 2). The most commonly used are these:

1. Written and published communication.
2. Oral public announcements.
3. Group presentations.
4. Performance appraisal.
5. Discussion of salary actions.

### EXHIBIT 2

### Basic Communication Methods

| Methods | Advantages | Disadvantages |
|---|---|---|
| Written and published communications | Documentation | Impersonal/legalistic |
| Oral public announcements | Efficient | Impersonal |
| Group presentations | Efficient | Impersonal |
| Performance appraisal | Direct | Overload—can be too stressful |
| Salary discussion | Direct | Overload—can be too stressful |

*Written and published communication* is the most obvious broadcast medium. Bulletin boards, newsletters of all sorts, company newspapers, letters to the employees, news releases to local newspapers, and the like are all representative of this type of communication. It is so prevalent that most organizations charge an individual on the staff with the responsibility for generating it. The relative ease and low cost with which written communication can be prepared, duplicated, and distributed make it a particularly good way of transmitting a great deal of information. The mere fact that the information has been put into writing and disseminated has the added advantage of providing documented proof of its availability. Anyone who doubts that the opening of the cafeteria has been announced can be shown a copy of the newsletter or bulletin in which the announcement was published.

Unfortunately, the flood of such materials has dulled the response of the typical employee, and he is likely to view it more as an impersonal method of telling him something than as an information service. At the same time, the tendency is to use each release as a semilegal document so that the employee who fails to "get the message" can be held personally responsible. This amounts to something of a latter-day *caveat emptor*, but now it is the reader who must beware lest he miss an item of importance in the stream of information directed to him. An unfortunate but typical employee response to this kind of policy is to ignore all messages. The strategy is a sound one: If most of the employees ignore all written communications, management can hardly single out any one individual for blame.

We must not forget that people can readily protect themselves from broadcast communication merely by turning off the receiver. Then it doesn't make any difference how much is transmitted through how many channels; with the receiver off, all messages are lost. This is obviously one of the most prevalent and nagging problems in developing an effective broadcast system for communication with employees.

*Oral public announcements and group presentations* also are frequently used. Some plants have public-address systems which are intended to reach every last employee in the organization; or, in the absence of such a system, employees may be called together in an auditorium or other area and addressed as a group. Still another plan which combines both oral and written communication, is to give all the line supervisors in the company a message to be read aloud at simultaneous departmental meetings. After reading the message, each supervisor explains its contents in simple terms and perhaps answers questions from the group.

Because it is hard for employees to ignore this kind of communication, such "captive audience" techniques are often used to insure that employees get management's message. However, anyone who has observed the resulting gatherings can cite ways in which people can avoid being involved or hearing what is being said: They go to sleep; they carry on whispered conversations; or they stare into space, their minds elsewhere. In short, the receiver is turned off, or it is turned so low that many of the messages come through badly distorted. Finally, even when the message is so simple, direct, and hard-hitting that no one can avoid hearing it, we need only listen to the reactions of employees as they leave the meeting to hear them express resentment at having been sat down and preached to. The manager who delivered the message is likely to be criticized for everything from his voice quality or his jokes to the color of his necktie.

This method of communication is, therefore, no panacea either.

*Performance appraisal* may not seem at first blush to be an appropriate technique for inclusion under the broadcast method of communication, but careful research shows that it is a typical sender-channel-receiver activity. Many articles and instruction manuals on the subject discuss in glowing terms the mutuality of the discussion, the high degree of agreement and understanding, and the other desirable results to be had from appraisals. In truth, however, a performance appraisal is essentially the boss's evaluation of a subordinate's work. The boss spells out what he likes and dislikes about the employee's performance and, in effect, tells him in what ways he is a good or a poor employee.

In one recent study, an effort was made to offset the weaknesses of appraisal based solely on the manager's judgment. To this end, each employee whose performance was to be evaluated was asked to develop a self-appraisal. It was thought that this might alter the direction of the flow of information between employee and manager and that greater candidness would result. But hopes were quickly dashed as the appraisal sessions were observed and analyzed. Although it was clear that self-appraisal was a refreshing experience for manager-employee pairs who had worked together for some time, it was also clear that judgments *were* being discussed and that the manager's estimate of the employee's performance dominated the exchange, no matter who initiated a particular point.

In the final analysis, the manager is in a position to give his employee help or to withhold it; he can strongly influence the employee's rate of progress and promotion. Also, he has what a sociologist would call "fate control"; that is, he has the power to reward or penalize according to his evaluation of the employee's performance. The result is that the employee *must know* what his manager expects of him and how his manager judges his work if he wants to get ahead. The employee who sits down in an appraisal session for the first time to hear his boss evaluate his performance *needs* to listen. The manager who is evaluating an employee for the first time can therefore be sure he is being heard with unusual sensitivity.

Performance appraisal is a useful method of transmitting information from manager to employee. There are, however, few if any such discussions in which two points of view are examined. Rather, everything else is put aside by both participants so that the one crucial point of view—the manager's—can be fully and completely understood.

Moreover, appraisal is no perfect tool even for communicating the manager's viewpoint. Research done in the General Electric Company indicates that it may give results that are diametrically opposed to what is intended. Instead of leading to improvement, it sometimes causes a decrease in the quality of performance. A clear-cut change *is* likely to occur after a highly critical appraisal, but this change is often for the worse.

What happens is so systematic and so obviously related to the appraisal that it cannot be dismissed as coincidence. The employee who is severely criticized by his manager during the appraisal tends to react defensively. In effect, he denies that his poor performance is his own fault. If the point is made that he is failing to meet schedules, he may miss even more schedules in the following weeks. It is as though he were saying, "You criticized me for not meeting schedules that I know I'm supposed to meet, but your criticism hasn't helped me meet them any better." Essentially, this is his attitude: "I have no control over the circumstances, and I should not be criticized for problems relating to them."

In summary, when an appraisal goes awry, when an employee feels he has been unjustly charged with too many failures or faults, something new happens in the manager/employee communication process. Some sort of response *is* elicited from the employee; as often as not, however, it is cryptic or symbolic rather than literal or direct.

In spite of all the criticism leveled at performance appraisal in recent years, however, it remains a necessary and useful technique of communication in the typical company and will remain so as long as that company is organized along hierarchical lines. It is no more than reasonable that an employee know what his manager expects of him and, indeed, that he be allowed to discover his manager's biases, standards, needs, demands, idiosyncrasies, strategies, and weaknesses. Only then can he logically be expected to perform to his manager's expectations and specifications.

*Salary discussion* is frequently just another form of appraisal, although recent research has shown that attempts to take up both needed performance improvements and salary in the same discussion nearly always fail. When a dollar value is being placed on a person's contribution to the organization, an agitated discussion usually ensues. Moreover, if an evaluation of the employee's performance is inferred in any salary action, that action performs almost the same function as appraisal.

Many salary increases have lately come to represent adjustments to the cost of living, or "a slice of the productivity pie," more than anything else. Employees tend to expect regular advances in wages regardless of performance. The evaluative aspect of salary action has therefore been severely diluted by other forces in the arena of wage economics. The result is considerable confusion. No one knows for certain what an increase in salary implies in terms of performance or individual worth to the organization. Thus it is not surprising that wage and salary administration is becoming one of the liveliest topics of discussion among employees and managers alike. The manner in which increases are determined and the treatment of differential work classifications in regard to salary are the subjects of endless debate.

The only logical explanation is that salary determination has become so complex and so symbolic that it is now a "safe" topic that can be discussed without fear of offending anyone. In fact, talk about salary administration and salary action between any two people in an organization, particularly manager and subordinate, is often something of a game. The fact that the employee pursues the game aggressively and that the manager is likely to be on the defensive suggests that the employee is attempting to initiate a dialogue. Unless the manager can participate in such a dialogue, he will be unable to come to grips with any of the underlying issues or arrive at any agreement—

except to specify that the talking is to stop until he is ready to communicate in depth with his employee.

## Total Reliance Unwise

Broadcast communication, then, serves a very useful and necessary role in business. It is a simple, inexpensive, and efficient means of disseminating messages to a large number of employees. The usual hierarchy of the organization sensitizes employees to messages from the top, and management can therefore transmit a great deal of information with relative ease.

The method has some distinct disadvantages, however. The manager who is insufficiently sensitive to people can provoke or alienate his listeners without knowing he has done so until it is too late. What is worse, messages circulated in this way may be interpreted by the employee as reminders that the manager is boss and that the employee has to take whatever the boss wants to dish out.

Each type of broadcast communication that has been discussed also has specific disadvantages of its own. Written material passed out to employees or posted on the bulletin board is impersonal and gives any message a distinctly mechanical flavor. As a result, it may well fail to capture the reader's attention. Oral announcements and group presentations suffer the same fate.

So far as performance appraisal or salary discussion is concerned, the greatest cause of failure is likely to be too much or too threatening a barrage of inputs. The employee perceives and reacts to these inputs as representing an evaluation of his worth, and that evaluation can be thoroughly demoralizing. If it is out of tune with his own evaluation of his worth, he must either accept his manager's judgment and change his view of himself or deny the validity of the judgment and build a set of defenses around his self-concept. In other words, either he knuckles under or he fights back. Of the two responses, the latter is probably the healthier for the employee, though it will cause greater problems for the appraising manager.

Broadcast communication fills a need, but total reliance on it is the mark of undeveloped managerial ability. Much more will be needed in the way of communicative techniques by the manager who wants to cope effectively with all the human and technical problems he faces.

# 7

—————————•◆•—————————

# *The Technical Model*
# *of Communication*

IN THE TECHNICAL FIELD of communication—that is, communications engineering—one of the earliest approaches to the problems of the sender-channel-receiver communications model was to examine qualities of the components to determine how these could distort the message. Thus the fidelity of the transmitter and receiver and the noise characteristics of the channel became the principal concerns of the communications engineer.

These are worthwhile concerns. That the characteristics of transmitter, channel, and receiver do have an effect on communication is beyond question, and these characteristics and their effects should definitely be taken into account in studying communication within organizations.

*Monitoring the Signals*

The principal difference between the basic and the technical models of broadcast communication lies, in fact, in these elements of the system. (See Exhibit 3.) With the technical model, the sender becomes acutely aware of his sending capabilities and the potential distortion in channel and receiver. He begins to monitor his own sig-

## EXHIBIT 3

## The Technical Model

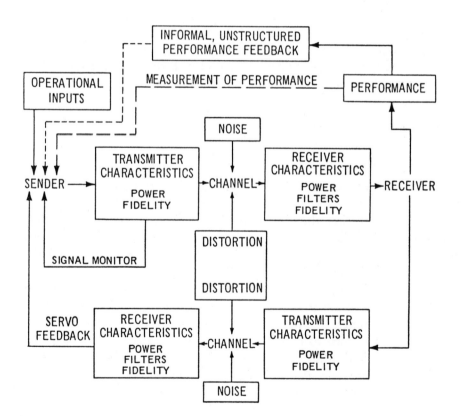

nals—that is, he obtains immediate feedback of what he is saying so that he can catch and clarify any ambiguities or inherent misunderstandings in his message.

The difference here is essentially the difference between naive messages that are full of ambiguities and double meanings as compared to skillful messages that are carefully framed in simple, precise terms and phrases which spell out the sender's meaning accurately. The skillful communicator is, for instance, aware that an article in a newspaper can contain a typographical error that distorts its meaning. He is aware that the communications medium he is using has inherent in it certain random noises that can destroy part or all of his message's content.

The receiver, of course, is beyond the direct control of the message sender. If, however, the sender has a basic knowledge of the characteristics of typical receivers, he can judge which messages are most likely to get through and which may be blocked or distorted. And this ability to discriminate between messages can be very valuable. By monitoring his own messages, by making it his business to be aware of the way his messages are received, the effective communicator is able to predict the response of his listeners.

## Redundancy and Its Use

The effective communicator also realizes that messages must be reiterated in order to insure clarity. For this purpose he makes use of *redundancy*.

In information theory, "redundancy" is the extent to which a signal repeats the same message. Thus the probability of error is reduced—although, at the same time, the effective capacity of the communications channel is reduced as well.

The typical course in public speaking enjoins the speaker to repeat the most important statements in his presentation, not once or twice, but several times. Each time he goes back over a key point, his audience has a chance to compare this hearing of the message with the last. Then, if the listener notices a difference between the two versions, he may realize that noise in the system kept him from receiving the message correctly the first time.

So it is with written communication. Suppose, for example, that wholesale layoffs of personnel are rumored. Knowing that the "noise" created by the company grapevine is likely to block messages from management, those responsible for healthy employee relations will have to find several ways of reiterating that any layoffs are temporary and confined to one department where the workload is slack; that orders for the company's existing products are bigger than ever; and that new products being developed will require additions to the workforce. Appropriate channels of communication may include the company newspaper, bulletin-board notices, letters to employees' homes—and, naturally, informal messages via first-line supervision.

## Increased Complexity

With the necessary awareness of his communication system, the communicator may be able to transmit information which is fairly complex in nature. He may, on the other hand, be restricted by the performance of the receiver. To progress much beyond the simplicity required by the basic broadcast model of communication, he must have access to reasonably reliable facts about the receiver. He may now, however, use performance measures that are not nearly so immediate or precise. If his knowledge of the communication system, including the receiver, gives him enough confidence that the desired message got through, he may be able to tolerate waiting for feedback to occur at some later time.

The shipping supervisor, for example, wants to be sure that an incoming shipment gets to the toolroom promptly. He tells an employee: "Be on the lookout for a shipment of tools from the Ace Tool Company—there's one due in the next day or so. When it arrives, let me know immediately." The supervisor in this instance is relatively safe in assuming that his message has gotten through, but he will do well to make sure that the employee can recognize a shipment from Ace Tool (Has he handled such shipments in the past? Is he familiar with the contents?) and can be relied on to follow instructions. Only when the supervisor's message is precise and immediately understandable, and he knows the channel is relatively distortion-free, can the message be received accurately and acted upon in a timely and appropriate fashion. This most efficient method of communicating is one that should produce excellent results—here, prompt notification on the part of the employee that the Ace tools have arrived on schedule.

Increasing the complexity of the message communicated will increase the likelihood of failure even with this advanced system. The supervisor tells a new employee in the shipping department: "Be on the lookout for poorly packaged supplies from the ABC Company." This is a very risky order if the employee has no standard against which to compare the quality of the packaging. If he is left to determine quality on his own, he may not know that he has to open the crate in order to determine whatever damage may have occurred as a result of defective packaging. Thus a large element of chance is built into the original message and the employee's response. The likelihood of reliable performance in this case is therefore 50–50 at best.

## The Matter of Filters

In general, the more complex the message transmitted on any one-way communication system, the less reliable its reception. This is the biggest problem with one-way communication: The receiver may be on or off, and there may be no way to tell which is the case except by the subsequent behavior of the receiver. Beyond this problem, however, is the need to take into account certain other receiver characteristics. Receivers may be high-fidelity or low-fidelity: They may be capable of reproducing an incoming signal either accurately or inaccurately. And, finally, they may have various filters built into the system intentionally or unintentionally.

The matter of filters should not be treated lightly. The employee who dislikes his manager is not likely to believe a communication from him about his benevolence or personal concern. Rather, the employee will filter the message and hear what he expected to hear, not what was intended. For instance, if he is reminded of the penalties for breaking specific rules, he may get the message that the manager is determined to catch him violating those rules.

Also, employees often seem to have filters that cut out the noise at both extremes of the frequency range—the sounds that are so subtle they can be ignored and the ones that are excessively loud. During a particularly critical performance appraisal, for instance, the subordinate may filter out the criticism by denying its validity and alleging, at least to himself, that the shortcomings being discussed are really not his fault.

## The Technical Model Applied

Every transmitter-channel-receiver system is, in short, subject to error in transmission. Furthermore, such error is the rule rather than the exception. The fact that most comedy is based on misunderstandings between people with different perspectives and perceptions should be ample warning that no matter how carefully you monitor the transmission process to insure accuracy, no matter how cautiously you choose the channel to insure clarity, and no matter how well you get to know the receiving apparatus in an effort to compensate for any of its inherent weaknesses, there are ample opportunities for misunderstanding.

In business it is in the nature of communication to be highly complex. To achieve full accuracy, something is needed beyond the one-way transmission of messages. Nevertheless, the technical system is necessary and useful in the day-to-day operation of an enterprise. How does it work out in common practice? Exhibit 4 indicates some obvious areas in which it is applied:

- ✧ Informal discussions.
- ✧ Continuous performance evaluations.
- ✧ Frequent planning discussions.
- ✧ Counseling sessions.
- ✧ Coaching.

*Informal discussions* are the lifeblood of business communication. They give both manager and employee an opportunity to maintain a continuing check on the direction and progress of activities within the work group from day to day. Informal discussions are even credited with establishing warm, candid, two-way communication. In light of the evidence, however, it is probably unwise to assume that merely getting a manager and employee to talk informally creates a two-way exchange.

The typical casual discussion goes somewhat as follows: The man-

# EXHIBIT 4

## Advanced Communication Methods

| Techniques | Advantages | Disadvantages |
|---|---|---|
| Informal discussions | Low key, opportunity to explore | May be too subtle |
| Sender communicates his information about receiver's performance to receiver continuously | Receiver knows where he stands | Engenders overdependency; often deteriorates into a "no news is good news" pact |
| Frequent planning and strategy discussions | Sense of participation | Time consuming |
| Counseling | Optimum performance or attitude change | Much expertise required of sender |
| Coaching | Optimum performance or attitude change | Much expertise required of sender |

ager asks the employee who is having trouble with a machine, "Did you try this? How did it work out?" The employee responds, "I can't seem to find out what's wrong." Usually, very little new information is elicited from the employee except in general terms. He seldom feeds back much more to his manager than, "I'm having trouble," or, "I'm having no trouble."

In effect, the manager's production goals are foremost. The employee is coping with the balky machine as best he can, using a trial-and-error method. Having registered the preliminary inputs from the employee, the manager waits to see whether the employee is really in trouble; then, as the situation seems to grow worse rather than better, the manager authorizes an appeal to the maintenance department. The typical man/manager discussion, in other words, is tightly restricted to the issue of the work and its continuance with the minimum possible down time. Any suggestion that the employee might himself repair the machine is generally frowned on.

Informal discussions are often rather subtle. In fact, managers sometimes become so devious in their attempts to influence their employees that their messages never get across. That the sales manager is genuinely critical of the job being done in a particular territory and would like to see certain procedures changed is not likely to be clear if he limits himself to suggesting, "Bill has had experience with this kind of promotion. You might check with him on it." What the manager intends to convey to the salesman is: "Bill knows the right way to promote this product line, and you don't. If you ask his advice, you may learn too." Because the manager failed to speak plainly, he is likely to be disappointed by the lack of an upward trend in sales. What the employee will probably hear in the ambiguous suggestion that he check with Bill is a request that he pay a duty call on Bill and talk over the current campaign. But, since Bill is not the boss, the salesman is free to ignore Bill's criticisms or suggestions. So the salesman's performance is no better than it was, and the manager has merely wasted his and Bill's time.

The lesson to be drawn from all this is that the manager who wants an employee to emulate the work of another has to make his message explicit. Even so, a great many issues can and should be handled through informal, low-key, general-purpose discussion.

*Continuous feedback about performance* is loudly touted as "the only way to appraise." The manager is warned that he should never wait a year, six months, or even three months to tell an employee whether he is performing well. Rather, as each day's work is completed, it is suggested that the manager ought to evaluate the quality of performance represented and make his evaluation known to the employee. The theory is that the employee should know exactly where he stands at all times.

Unfortunately, two undesirable side effects can often be observed. First, the employee is encouraged to be overdependent. He quickly learns that he can avoid criticism by obtaining an evaluation of his methods in advance. In essence, the employee asks the manager for detailed instructions on how to do the job and then restricts himself to merely carrying out those instructions. Any point that is at all unclear to him he promptly takes up with the manager to determine what the latter would do. Then the manager's instructions are followed to the letter.

In these circumstances, it is hardly surprising if the manager is pleased with the results. It is, after all, almost as though he were doing the job himself; and, if he considers himself an expert in the work, what could be better than to have the employee do it in exactly the boss's way? This arrangement may be tolerable for a while or—provided the manager can devote a great deal of time to laying work out for the employee—even indefinitely. However, in situations where the employee should be at least as capable a problem solver as his manager, it will be at best a waste of the manager's time.

The second undesirable side effect of the continuous appraisal is the probability of a "no news is good news" pact. Many man/manager pairs fall into a pattern of never communicating unless something is wrong. The employee operates almost autonomously, and only the more serious problems are discussed on a real-time basis. The employee quickly learns what disturbs his manager or elicits his criticism and proceeds to build the necessary defenses to avoid the obvious traps. He may even succeed in making himself immune to criticism. In the long run, however, manager and employee merely cut themselves off from one another and can even cut themselves off from change.

Continuous appraisal between man and manager can be effective where an exceptionally good relationship exists from the beginning. Otherwise, the inevitable little day-to-day ploys which every employee knows how to use are likely to make the pattern deteriorate into one that neither the employee nor the manager really wants.

*Frequent work-planning sessions* are perhaps the most popular new wrinkle in man/manager communication. The idea is to formulate plans and goals with the employee's participation and concurrence. The chief merit of the technique is involvement of the employee before he does the work that will be required of him, at a time when variations in the plans are still possible, so that he will not be in the position of having to implement plans to which he has not agreed but, on the contrary, will be motivated to achieve the goals he has helped to establish.

In its most sophisticated form, work planning is used by large firms in developing specific goals for their major components along with measures of profit, sales, and return on investment. Managers have a high degree of autonomy in deciding what operating strategy to pursue—as long as they are able to meet their goals. To a certain extent, some of this autonomy may be available—and desirable—for nonmanagerial employees as well. And perhaps not only managers but employees too should have goals to pursue, specific measures of achievement, and permission to apply any operating strategies or techniques they think are appropriate.

There are some problems here, of course. First, not many jobs lend themselves to the setting of requirements in such general terms that wide flexibility is possible in the choice of work methods. Many jobs, even those of high-level managers, are routinized and governed by prescribed procedures. There may be a small amount of freedom as regards the artfulness or variation with which the employee *applies* the customary techniques, but in most organizations the techniques themselves are firmly established and are, for all practical purposes, mandatory. When a great many decisions about the conduct of the job are needed from the employee, something other than the broadcast or technical model of direct communication should be used.

Hence the value of work planning, which is an excellent way of working out objectives for complex tasks. When, however, the task is more than merely routine, careful advance definition is essential to insuring its successful completion, and work planning as it is currently practiced often falls short of this ideal. Usually, a detailed set of specifications is prepared by the manager for the individual employee; and, while discussion of these specifications may give the employee an opportunity to make suggestions for incorporation into the work plan, it would be naive to assume that the work will be done in a way that does not conform to the manager's wishes.

Admittedly, work planning holds the potential for facilitating two-way communication with employees. If for no other reason than this, it should be practiced.

The *counseling session* is similar to the informal discussion between manager and employee except that it is more likely to deal with subjects such as level of skill or employee attitude rather than with those that are more directly related to the job.

Many managers do an excellent job as "directive" counselors. They listen to their employees' problems and prescribe courses of corrective action in much the same way that a doctor prescribes a rest cure or a medicine. If a boss is skilled in arriving at his diagnoses and formulating his prescriptions, and if he has enough concern for his employees, he may develop a reputation as a fine manager and so be able to do an effective job of training and development. But it should be noted that a great deal of experience as well as expertise is necessary to become a successful counselor and that not every manager has the necessary aptitude. The neophyte counselor is all too ready to preach a resounding sermon—an approach which often elicits a negative rather than a positive reaction. In contrast, the manager who learns how to make sound but cautious suggestions on the basis of considerable experience with similar problems can be a great help to his employees and an asset to his organization.

*Coaching* might be termed just another form of counseling, except that it deals more directly with performance. The new employee who is being coached carries out an assignment under the watchful eye of his supervisor or an experienced worker and is corrected as he goes along. This combination—immediate pinpointing of errors plus explanation of the correct way to do the job—is a highly effective technique for improving employee performance, but it requires considerable sensitivity. The good coach must be patient, but he must have high standards and insist that they be met. He must be careful never to criticize the employee himself; rather, he points out specific elements of the employee's performance which are in need of correction.

Effective as coaching can be, it is still one-way communication wherein the manager, relying on a fund of experience and expertise, observes performance and prescribes changes which will improve it. The manner in which these prescriptions are delivered is crucial. If the manager is critical, evaluative, or judgmental, the effort may become no more than an appraisal of performance. If, on the other hand, his comments are supportive, appreciative, and respectful of the employee, they can be immensely effective.

## Needed: Direct Involvement

All these methods of communication have one serious flaw: They assume that the manager or supervisor always has the right answer at his fingertips. Whenever he is called on for help, he is expected to respond without delay and to communicate directly and meaningfully with his subordinate.

Although many managers would like to believe this is the way the business world operates, such a concept is hopelessly unrealistic. Every manager encounters problems to which he does not have the answers; that's why he is provided with staff assistance in marketing, purchasing, finance, personnel, and the rest. Yet staff assistance may not suffice; many problems cannot be solved except with the cooperation of one's subordinates. When they are the only people who possess the specialized knowledge, experience, or understanding that are needed, some way *must* be found to elicit their involvement.

The methods outlined so far are excellent for directing the activities of employees up to, but not including, the point of enlisting their active and wholehearted assistance. At that point these techniques fall woefully short of the mark. Something much better than the one-way communication model or even the highly sophisticated technical model is needed to draw the employee into the problem-solving process. We are therefore faced with a dilemma: The traditional methods used in discussions between managers and employees can discourage employee involvement. The manager is still invested with "fate control" over the employee, and the penalty of being misunderstood may still exceed the rewards of being understood.

What to do? Certainly, whatever more is done, we must consider the problem of communication, not from the standpoint of directing the activities of employees, but from that of participation in problem solution.

# 8

—————— ➤ ◆ ◄ ——————

## *Feedback:*

## *The Loop Closed*

AT THIS POINT let us summarize some of the communication principles which we have already discussed:

1. Business organizations are constructed along hierarchical lines designed to insure optimum sensitivity among people at lower levels to communication from higher levels. The unfortunate corollary to this pattern is that sensitivity to upward communication can be, and often is, minimal.
2. Attempts by employees to communicate upward can be fraught with peril. Should a subordinate try to make his point of view heard and be misunderstood, the responsibility for the error can too easily be placed on him. In some organizations, the penalties are so great that it does not pay

to try to communicate upward unless there is no other choice.

3. The manager in a man/manager relationship can cut off communication arbitrarily if he finds it offensive. This can be a severe punishment; being refused recognition can be totally devastating.

4. Most business communication is highly directive; that is, it is designed to influence behavior very precisely toward organizational goals and purposes. However, it thereby discourages the potential contributions of subordinates to solving the problems of the firm. As often as not, the initiative for generating upward communication lies with the employee: He will communicate to the extent that he is willing to insert himself into the process of problem solution, although only the most aggressive or ambitious employee is likely to take the risk. The great majority of people sit quietly on the sidelines waiting for management to stumble onto the right solution—which may be painfully obvious to these same employees.

## Lessons in Failure

Having invested so much time, skill, and energy in insuring that downward communication is being attended to by employees, how can we surmount the barriers to upward communication and begin to elicit needed employee contributions? Or are we doomed to failure?

Important lessons can be learned from any failure, and one of the central lessons about communication is to be found in one of America's greatest military disasters—Pearl Harbor. Information which should have alerted every military commander in the Pacific Theater to an impending attack was in the hands of the chief of staff, General George C. Marshall, two hours earlier. However, War Department radio contact with Hawaii had been lost that morning, and General Marshall's subordinates, rather than disturb him with such "trivia," ordered that the message be transmitted to Hawaii by commercial teletype.

In one man's view, General Marshall "failed to require surveillance and positive report on the delivery of his final warning"[1] to military commanders in the Pacific, and the message arrived *after* the attack. According to others, the most important reason for the disaster at Pearl Harbor was "the fact that decisions were made on a unilateral basis and communications followed a single channel."[2]

Clearly, there are times when the broadcast model of communication can be disastrous. Something more is needed.

## The Servo-System

The solution would appear to be the introduction of man/manager communication techniques which will elicit *feedback* from employees.

The engineers have a word for it: They call it a "servo-system." By this they mean a system that constantly monitors itself at the receiving end of the message channel. The transmitted message is not merely received, it is immediately sent back to the source, where the message as retransmitted is compared with the original to determine whether the output of the system is right. Any error is corrected at once.

Exhibit 5 illustrates in simple form the servo-system or problem-solving model of communication. As indicated, the only real difference between the models that were discussed earlier and this new model is that the new one has built into it the capacity for communicating *in both directions.*

In its simplest form, this model operates in the following way: The manager states the problem and tentatively defines the goals which, if reached, should provide a satisfactory solution. Thus:

> Down time on the No. 5 production line has soared to 36 percent. At that rate we're losing money on that line—we've got to do something about it. We can't quite put our finger on the trouble, but it seems that the machines break down too often because they're being operated improperly. We're not sure whether it's intentional,

---

[1] T. N. Dupuy, "Pearl Harbor—Who Blundered?" *American Heritage*, Vol. 13, No. 2, February, 1962.
[2] Rocco Carzo, Jr. and John N. Yanouzas, *Formal Organization: A System Approach*, Richard D. Irwin, Inc., Homewood, Ill., 1967, p. 441.

## EXHIBIT 5

### The Servo-System

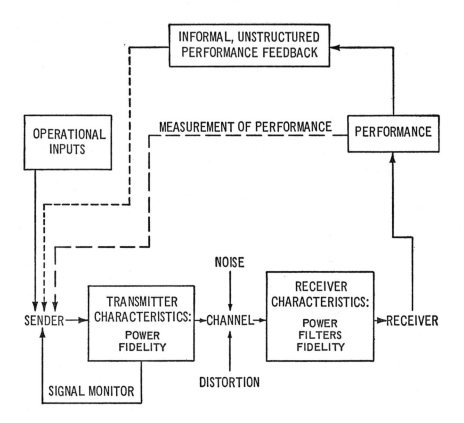

just a matter of improper training, or something else. How do we go about finding out?

Here we have the problem stated in the most general and tentative terms. The responsible manager takes care to be as explicit as possible about its elements and to avoid jumping to conclusions. He wisely refrains from taking a directive role because of his limited knowledge and because he understands that, if he begins directing a concerted effort to "find out why those dumb guys can't operate their machines right," he puts himself in the position of having to have all the right answers from the start. His subordinates will be unlikely to provide any answers at all if he expresses himself in a highly dogmatic way. He doesn't want to be the sort of manager who looks for a scapegoat or who has preconceptions about the performance of the employees on the No. 5 line. Quite the contrary. To make upward communication easier, he rejects the traditional managerial approach, which makes a great display of confidence and is designed to get results by frightening subordinates into activity.

## The Steps in Sequence

Our revised system, then, begins with a message which permits a *broad range of response from the employee.* It carries no hint of severe penalty, of anger, or of lack of confidence disguised behind a reassuring mask. Rather, the initial message is open and presumes little or nothing.

The next step is for the manager to invite feedback: "I know that a lot of things could be going wrong and that you're closer to the problem than I am. What's your analysis of it?" With such a statement the manager invites the employee to say what he thinks the problem is and to make any suggestions which may be helpful in working toward the solution.

The third step in the process is vital. Having opened the door to the employee by asking for his cooperation, the manager must now be alert to any fears the employee may have about getting himself into trouble. In other words, it is still all too likely that the employee will avoid becoming involved in an evaluation of the problem but will instead try to "read" his manager so as to identify *his* biases and preconceptions.

Assume the employee says, "I don't really have any ideas at all. What do *you* think?" The manager then knows immediately that the employee is unwilling to try to solve the problem, is genuinely unable to solve it, or is avoiding any personal commitment until he is sure the manager can tolerate inputs from a subordinate. At this point, the manager's effectiveness as a communicator is called into fullest play.

He must give the employee every opportunity to test the validity of the invitation to make suggestions while simultaneously leaving him a way to escape gracefully in case he is unwilling or unable to contribute to the problem's solution.

Such a determination, however, would appear to be crucial; a manager must learn the extent of his employees' abilities sooner or later if he is to help them develop or recommend them for promotion. He will be wise to test as early as possible their self-confidence, their willingness to be open and candid in communicating with him, and their capacity for taking risks. These secondary outcomes are as worthwhile as the primary outcome of problem solution, and they make it all the more important to use the problem-solving, or systems, approach to communication.

When the employee finally offers his suggestions about the production-line problem, the next critical point is reached: It is essential that his inputs be treated with the greatest respect even if the manager's first reaction is that they are implausible or impractical. The manager must be capable of at least thinking, if not saying, "I may be wrong in my assessment of this problem. I'd better hear him out." This is an intelligent assumption for him to make at this juncture; his subordinates must believe that if he knew the solution to the problem he could merely give orders instead of asking for advice. "Our manager is human," they must be able to reason, "and, like most managers, he is not sure he does have the right solution. He is therefore willing to explore every possibility, even those which run contrary to his own predispositions or biases or which he finds personally disconcerting."

Suppose the employee suggests: "I don't think of operating skill as the problem on that line. The way it looks to me—and I've heard some of the other guys say this too—the materials coming onto the line are some of the poorest I've ever seen. A lot of our down time may be the result of substandard materials jamming in the machines." Our manager now has an alternate hypothesis. It may be difficult to do anything about it if his best friend, who happens to be the inspector, has long since assured him that substandard materials could not possibly slip by, but the manager must hold friendship in abeyance while considering his problem. His reaction may be: "That's silly. I know the inspector of incoming materials. He wouldn't let anything like that happen!" In that case he destroys any further opportunity to get more of the employee's inputs and so move into a problem-solving, or systems, approach to communication.

## The Secret to Problem-Solving Success

If there is a secret to the problem-solving model of communication, it is this: Fair and respectful treatment of every suggestion, even those that are personally repugnant or seem too far out to be acceptable when first presented. The manager who always snorts gruffly, "That doesn't make any sense!" will never be able to obtain the cooperation of his employees. They will not communicate their own perceptions of problems for fear of being cut down.

Welcoming what seem at times to be "oddball" solutions and being willing to explore them fully constitute one cost of this approach to communication with subordinates. Initially, it may seem a relatively high investment for the manager. He may have to allow his subordinates to test him so that they can see how sincere he really is in inviting their assistance. But, if he can tolerate being sent on a wild-goose chase or two without getting upset, he may begin to get genuinely useful inputs from his people. He must—to repeat—get down off his high horse as much as necessary to make the system work. For it is a simple fact that people will not be candid about what they think or feel until their trust is won.

In today's business organizations, moreover, a problem-solving approach is often the only one that can succeed. Direct, open two-way communication is essential, for instance, among the company's managers of finance, marketing, and manufacturing. If they are unable to speak frankly with one another about their mutual problems, they will be unable to solve them. Many elements of modern business are so complex, and such a high degree of specialized skill and knowledge is required to carry them out successfully, that it is nearly impossible for any manager—no matter how technically proficient—to direct the work in full. Cooperation and teamwork are critical to the success of the enterprise.

The engineer who must solve a design problem having to do with a rocket engine is not likely to receive precise directions for arriving at a solution. Similarly, on a more prosaic level, the salesman who is instructed to land a particularly big account may be given certain budget limitations, but otherwise he must work out a successful strategy on his own. By the time the sale is completed or lost, it will be too late to do anything about it, simply because the salesman's performance cannot be monitored directly. And, although the final outcome is evident (either he got the sale or he didn't), other crucial elements of performance in the sales area are not so easily observable: Has the salesman been maintaining customer goodwill? Has he been building up confidence in the company or in himself alone? If the salesman sells himself at the expense of the company, his performance in the short run may be good, but in the long run it will prove most unacceptable.

The only way the manager can get around problems of this sort is to have lines of communication with the employee open enough that even so serious a practice as disparaging the company to make a sale can be discussed frankly. Such disparagement may be a reasonable tactic if the sale is that important, but hiding it from management afterward could have quite undesirable results in that other employees, who might occasionally want to use extreme measures in the achievement of goals, would be afraid to incur management's displeasure. Yet management might tolerate such extremes if it knew about them and were in a position to offset any negative side effects. What is needed, clearly, is communication with full feedback.

## The Communication Catalyst

In all situations where the information to be transmitted is highly complex and likely to be misinterpreted by the employee, or where information about performance may be unavailable to the manager except through the employee, the only method of communication that can work is the systems model with the feedback loop firmly and securely in place.

This is well illustrated by a technique that is currently popular in settling labor-management disputes. The technique is simple, although applying it takes a great deal of skill. As long as both parties to the dispute accept the need to improve their relationship, it is possible for a neutral third party—a "communication catalyst," we shall call him—to assist the two principals by establishing and enforcing one simple ground rule: Every time a participant speaks, he must begin by summarizing the points made by the previous speaker—to the complete satisfaction of that speaker. In other words, no one is permitted to make his own point until he demonstrates that he has been listening to the messages from the other side of the table.

The effect of this simple prescription can be dramatic. For the first time, the disputants are *required* to receive the messages their adversaries are transmitting. Generally, each side discovers that it has had its transmitter turned on full blast but that its receiver has been turned off. Points of concurrence have been overlooked because they were not heard. Now, with two-way communication enforced, differences are narrowed until, finally, only the fundamental ones stand exposed for examination by all concerned. Having been identified, they can be dealt with in some sensible, systematic, and rational way.

What has happened? The bombast has been abandoned, and this is perhaps the most important step toward solving deep-rooted problems in labor-management relations or any other type of human activity. As soon as the disputing parties get past the stage of trying to overwhelm one another with words, they can begin communicating.

To be sure, the technique has only been outlined here, and the role of the communication catalyst is very delicate, to say the least. However, the manager who applies this negotiating device in communicating with his people will in the long run be a far more effective manager and problem solver.

## Applications of the Systems Approach

What managerial processes lend themselves to the systems approach to communication? There are a number of interesting applications (see Exhibit 6). Few of them are really new, but all offer possibilities.

*Self-appraisal.* This is not a particularly novel device, but some fresh perspectives are now available on it. In brief, it has been suggested that self-appraisal might well be a way to avoid the problems inherent in having a manager level criticism at an employee in an appraisal discussion. Instead of requiring the manager to summarize the employee's contribution to the organization, the process is

# EXHIBIT 6

## Two-Way Communication Techniques

| Techniques | Advantages | Disadvantages |
|---|---|---|
| Self-appraisal | Establishes a feed-back loop | Uncomfortable to employee |
| Work planning and review | Work oriented | Time consuming |
| Career counseling | Opens door to employee's needs | Difficult to pull off |
| Questionnaires | Efficient, specific | Impersonal, often too specific |
| Morale interviews | Permits catalytic intervention | Increases the complexity of the system |
| All | | If applied as if they are "broadcast" or "technical" models, they won't work |

reversed. The employee is encouraged to open up and present his point of view.

True, a systematic examination of the self-appraisal method reveals that, by and large, it produces nothing more than a parroting back to the manager of the performance standards he has provisionally outlined. An employee who is asked to appraise his own performance without any sort of formal appraisal from his manager generally finds the process extremely uncomfortable. He may say, "I don't know what he wants of me." On the other hand, the employee who has had a comprehensive appraisal of his performance from his manager finds the process of self-appraisal refreshing. He can decide for himself the order in which various aspects of his performance are to be discussed and so bring out certain issues which he has been unable or unwilling to raise in the past. Self-appraisal, in effect, becomes a way of probing for the manager's reaction in areas which have not been clear to the employee.

For the manager, self-appraisal is equally refreshing. He finds himself more relaxed, with no sense of having a burden on his shoulders which must be transferred to the employee. He is in a position to accept or correct the employee's self-evaluation and, in the process, either verify the employee's perceptions or correct his *misperceptions* of what is desired of him. A self-appraisal is, in effect, a way of solving any erroneous interpretations of messages that may have been communicated in past appraisals.

The simple expedient of asking an employee to develop and deliver a self-evaluation, therefore, is an almost sure-fire method of immediately installing a feedback loop in the manager/employee communication system. It appears to be a vital first step toward the systems approach to communication; however, it would be a mistake to assume that merely installing a feedback loop corrects all the ills inherent in any man/manager relationship. There can be little doubt that, when first employed, self-appraisal is little more than a reflection of the manager's point of view of employee performance. In other words, the employee will probably evaluate his performance the way he feels his manager would evaluate it. An employee can get through a self-appraisal without once revealing how he himself feels about his job, his performance, or the opportunities for improving his contribution to the business. He may, nevertheless, use it as a way of probing areas of particular concern to him; and a perceptive and sensitive manager may, by watching for such probings, be able to identify these areas and subsequently encourage more extensive exploration.

The key is *encouragement*. To repeat: The manager must never forget that he has fate control over the employee and that a wise employee will not raise issues to which his manager might react negatively. The manager must demonstrate his tolerance to inputs from the employee before the inputs will be forthcoming.

*Work planning and review* (see also Chapter 7). One of the newer methods of man/manager communication, work planning—as we have seen—is based on the discovery that achievement is more likely to follow when a manager and employee agree upon specific goals than when the manager merely gives orders and from time to time criticizes the way in which the employee is doing his job. Work planning helps break the old habit of looking toward the past with a fault-finding attitude; instead, it encourages the habit of looking toward the future from a what-to-do-and-how-to-do-it point of view.

The manager begins by asking the employee to work out a set of detailed goals and plans for his job and bring them in for discussion on a specific date. At the appointed time, the manager and employee together review the goals and plans in detail and evaluate their relevance to business needs. A thorough discussion can lead to an improved understanding of the job's requirements and the methods by which those requirements may best be fulfilled.

It has already been pointed out that one of the principal disadvantages of this device is that a great many positions in business are not amenable to discretionary planning. A secretary, for example, must wait for the work to come to her before she can do it. She may have some flexibility in scheduling her typing or cleaning out her files, but she must respond immediately and appropriately when she is called on to take dictation, when the phone rings, or when someone comes to her desk. Her principal goal is to survive the hour-to-hour and day-to-day pressures that go with her job.

Thus work planning is genuinely applicable only in jobs where the employees' independent contributions are essential to the successful accomplishment of the work at hand. And it is precisely these positions that demand the most thorough and effective employee/manager communication. Failure to spell out the job and its specifications correctly may mean days or weeks of lost effort. Any misunderstanding of the job to be done, the goals to be met, and the methods of pursuing those goals must be identified and resolved in order to insure effective performance.

Work planning can be a very successful way of improving communication between a manager and his subordinate. It is job and task oriented, as well as future oriented, and it gives both men a sense of dealing with important issues. On the other hand, it is time consuming (though not nearly as time consuming as poor performance based on a poorly conceived plan), and it requires that the employee expose his personal point of view of the job to an extraordinary extent. Some people, moreover, perceive work planning and review as just another way to get more work for the same pay.

When first trying to implement work planning, therefore, it should come as no surprise that many of the plans drawn up by the employee are sketchy. It is as though he were holding himself back. He chooses goals which are so general as to be meaningless or so specific as to be trivial. In discussing his work, he fails to come to grips with the real problems. His plans for accomplishment are too superficial or incomplete to be useful, or they are limited to a simple statement of commitment to meet some goal by a particular date.

Another individual may formulate goals which are impossible to measure or even observe. For example, an employment interviewer sets as his objective "the improvement of the company's image with candidates for employment" and lines out tactics for making a better impression on job applicants. But how can he measure his relative success or failure? His manager might point out that it would be better to concentrate on goals that are measurable and can be reasonably expected to improve a prospective employee's impression of the company. The interviewer might then suggest, say, a 25 percent reduction in the time required to screen, test, and interview a job applicant. Or he might set up a goal calling for him to coach his interviewers and preliminary screeners in the techniques of processing candidates and, later on, check for improvement in those techniques. Or he might send out questionnaires to job candidates asking for their impressions of the company.

In the development of goals and plans, the crucial point is whether or not satisfactory measures of accomplishment can be agreed upon. Good work plans are amenable to observation and measurement in a way that makes sense to manager and employee alike. This is not to say that the manager's judgment of the employee's performance, as derived through direct observation, is not relevant. The average employee recognizes and accepts that judgment except in situations where he is unable to understand how and why it was formed. In this respect, the great strength of work planning and review lies in the fact that, in advance of achievement, both manager and employee can discover and accept a need for the manager's subjective evaluation as the final criterion of achievement. Reaching this kind of agreement can be a truly propitious event in the process of improving man/manager communication.

*Career counseling* (see also Chapter 7). Here is another effective way of establishing two-way communication between manager and employee. Research in motivation and employee turnover is beginning to develop some very useful findings on the relationship between career goals and individual motivation. The evidence is that the individual who has reached his level of aspiration is unlikely to expend much more than the most modest effort to progress any further; instead, the drive to continue advancing drops off sharply. Communication at this level between manager and subordinate is typically relaxed, with both parties aware of the lack of tension in the employee.

For a man on his way up, however, the drive to advance in status and salary can be intense, even though this is not always immediately apparent to his manager. This employee is likely to be something of an enigma; the manager may have the greatest difficulty in initiating communication with him. One reason for this difficulty is the fact, already cited, that most employees quickly learn to keep their own counsel and avoid taking risks until the manager has committed himself about the future. The manager who decides that an employee is unrealistic about his aspirations can blackball him for future promotion—or at least make the likelihood remote—by taking a strong stand to the effect that the employee is unqualified to advance. The employee therefore moves cautiously through this dangerous area, constantly on the lookout for signs of appreciation or criticism and keeping his hopes largely to himself. If he finds cues to the future, he tries to determine their implications on his own. If he does not, he eventually moves on to a new position in the hope of finding them there.

The manager who is aware of this drive and is willing to initiate a frank but respectful discussion of the employee's chances of getting ahead, as well as of his need for development, can tap a tremendous reservoir of productive energy. The employee who feels that his manager is looking out for his interests will give more than is called for in his job. Over and above this, however, the employee who is convinced that his manager is looking out for his personal interests will communicate openly and candidly. For these reasons, skilled career counseling between manager and employee can be the open sesame of problem-solving, systems-oriented communication.

Career counseling is seldom used in business because of the misconception that the manager must do the job as a trained vocational counselor might. There is a mistaken assumption that, in order to counsel employees about their careers and their potential for advancement, one must know how to make professional diagnoses of their aptitudes and interests and state authoritatively what they are best suited to do. The manager who conceives of the process in this way naturally feels unequal to it. Even trained vocational counselors have difficulty pulling it off—in fact, it is doubtful whether anyone is really capable of judging another's interests and aptitudes so precisely as to lay out an exact, infallible plan for his future.

The manager who avoids talking about careers with his employees for fear that he will be unable to do such precise planning is probably a good deal more realistic than the manager who falls into the trap of thinking he can study his people and prescribe just how far they can and will advance. Without question, some people consider the bestowal of managerial authority as a license to "play God." But the manager who tries it is likely to motivate his employees only to protect themselves from him at all costs and to find a new job as quickly as possible.

In a business setting, career counseling should be limited to providing those broader perspectives which the manager's longer experience and higher position give him, and which can be expected to assist an employee in estimating his chances for advancement. The manager who is an effective user of human resources should, in the first place, know the career paths available to his people and the opportunities for advancement both inside and outside his organization. Armed with this knowledge, the manager who seeks to counsel an employee will explore that employee's interests, aspirations, and goals and then try to provide a range of factual information about the possibilities of achieving those goals. When such information is missing, the manager will track it down. It may even be possible, once an individual's goals are outlined, for the manager to compare the skills needed to achieve those goals and the employee's existing skills and to counsel him on his developmental needs. This kind of counseling is, of course, the riskiest of all, and the manager should be aware of the availability of professional assistance.

The manager who knows from personal experience what is involved in getting ahead will not neglect to identify both the paths and the barriers to future promotion. The discussion need not end in an in-depth, authoritative, all-encompassing statement of how far the employee can expect to go and how he will get there. The effective manager/counselor is smart enough to listen intently and then spell out the realities of the promotional system as even the most highly trained vocational counselor cannot do. He does not pretend to be an expert in all phases of promotion; if he cannot answer certain questions, he admits his need to explore the subject further—and is alerted to areas that he probably should be examining.

The openness required on both sides, the lack of pat answers, and the potential spontaneity—all of which are inherent in a thorough discussion of career aspirations and promotional possibilities—provide a rich opportunity to open up a genuine two-way communication system between manager and employee. Such a discussion may, indeed, be the acid test of the manager's ability to listen and defer judgment in areas where he might normally jump to conclusions. Make no mistake about it: Career counseling requires not only extensive experience but a measure of self-confidence and a realistic view on the manager's part as to what career advancement is all about—qualities which are basic to effective two-way communication in any event.

*Morale interviews.* These have been used irregularly by personnel specialists and outside consultants for some time. They probably have limited application because they require a very high level of skill and, besides, the typical manager is in no position to evaluate the skill level of those who do the job for him. The safest route is usually to work with an experienced, reputable consulting firm.

Morale interviews perhaps have the greatest payoff and utility in situations where communication has been so bad that outside help is required. The real contribution of a consulting firm that undertakes internal morale interviewing is to provide a channel of communication where none exists. On a temporary basis, the consulting firm serves as a communication intermediary. It listens to the messages that go down through channels and evaluates their precision, ambiguity, and general comprehensibility. It listens to the employees to learn their needs and concerns and find out which of these are most consistently thwarted. Then it attempts to help management make itself better understood and to understand the concerns of the employees.

The firm which does this job well acts as a feedback loop in the communication system. To the extent that it can establish its credibility and trustworthiness, it may in a short time achieve a significant improvement in the communication climate of the organization. For, even when it is principally the technical know-how of the consulting firm which has been called upon, the communication role is at least as important as the technical. Indeed, the popularity of consulting firms in business probably rests more on their ability to open supplementary lines of communication than on any other function they perform.

Yet this process need not be limited to outside consultants. In many organizations, people who are particularly good listeners and who are generally well thought of can provide the supplementary channel of communication needed to solve particular problems. This is, of course, a difficult role to play; the individual must be capable of taking a broad view of the needs of the organization and avoid becoming involved in partisan squabbles along the way. He must be able to listen to bitter recriminations and still talk to each party objectively, without impairing his relationship with either. The individual who can do all this impartially and comfortably, keeping the best interests of the company in mind, can perform an invaluable service.

Unfortunately, the role is generally an accidental one. Few managers seek out and develop people with these capabilities or set aside any place for them in the organization. Logically, they might fit well in the personnel department—though not, of course, if the department is principally dedicated to fighting a union or penalizing managers for failing to do their administrative homework. It would seem reasonable, nonetheless, for a good personnel group to serve as a catalyst of effective communication throughout the entire organization.

*Attitude surveys.* An effective personnel department, moreover, should include an individual who is competent to prepare, administer, analyze, and feed back the results of extensive employee questionnaire surveys. The well-constructed and creatively conducted employee questionnaire can become an exceptionally valuable feedback loop in the total communication system. Handled competently, it should enable management to anticipate and solve human relations problems both promptly and efficiently.

## The Key Element

Clearly, the key to building a problem-solving systems model of communication in an organization or a manager/employee relationship is the feedback loop. Without some means of getting messages back from the other end of the channel, the opportunity for misunderstanding is just too great. All the techniques to be used in the development of the model must obviously, therefore, emphasize the feedback element.

Provision of a feedback loop, however, does not necessarily guarantee good communication. There must be a mutuality of understanding which can come about only through trust, which in turn is based on candidness. If work planning is being used solely to get more out of employees for the same pay, it will lead to poorer communication in the long run. If self-appraisal is being used solely to trap the employee into commitments he really does not want to make, it will lead to distrust and impairment of communication. Only when the manager demonstrates sincere respect and interest in the employee's point of view can communication begin to open up.

The typical manager, confronted with these facts, complains loudly that he hasn't enough time for "all that." In truth, he may not. He may be so busy trying to know all the answers and direct all the work in his department that he has no time to find out what his employees think about his decisions. And, so long as he knows everything that is going on and has a solution to every problem, perhaps he really doesn't need to worry about feedback or improved communication with his people.

To the extent that the manager can tell someone precisely what he is to do and then determine whether he does it satisfactorily, it may be unimportant to know whether the employee likes doing it. However, when the work becomes too complicated to direct in this way or too intangible to measure precisely, the name of the game changes quickly. It is no longer enough to be the benevolent autocrat. Effective communication and effective problem solving may be the only techniques which will enable the manager to survive.

## Beyond Inaccuracies in Communication

The question now arises: Can we solve all our problems merely by insuring that we get adequate feedback from our communications? Can we, by simply monitoring the interpretation of all our messages at the receiving end, guarantee that no problems will arise in our relationships with the listener? As long as the manager is certain that what he is saying is fully understood by his subordinates, shouldn't he be able to handle any problem merely by making sure that a feedback loop exists?

It is certainly true that when communication is garbled or misunderstood by the receiver, solving problems of any sort is next to impossible. A failure to see that a feedback loop is in place is likely to cause insurmountable obstacles. Only in the improbable event that messages are understood perfectly can a problem be dealt with adequately in the absence of feedback. If manager and employee are talking about the same thing, they are on the way to a solution of some sort; if they are talking about two different things, they are worlds apart in working toward any solution. And, lacking a feedback loop, total agreement is a matter of chance.

But there is more to problem solving than feedback. To be sure, many problems involve simple misunderstandings; and as quickly as these can be reconciled, the two parties can perhaps recognize that they are working toward the same objectives and have merely been talking about them in different terms. What happens, however, when, having come to a common understanding, the two discover that their objectives are diametrically opposed?

Not all human problems involve mere semantic differences. A good many involve basic disagreements as to human values. For instance, what do you do when you, as a supplier, discover that your customer is out to get the best possible price whether you make or lose money on the deal? This is a fundamental issue: One party is pursuing his self-interest in single-minded fashion while the other is attempting to bridge the existing differences and retain the customer's goodwill and friendship.

People who play "cutthroat" in this way often lose their friends and end up with nobody to do business with. In day-to-day relationships, most of us are less determinedly blunt in our approach, but our perspective is nonetheless selfish. So how do we get one another to see and appreciate our point of view?

To begin with, sometimes it may be impossible to get the other person to agree that our point of view, although different from his own, has validity. When this happens, the solution is to withdraw; to get out of his way and leave him to himself. If he doesn't want to be left alone and wants your company or your assistance, he must re-open the relationship on a new basis. In other words, the differences between people can never be resolved as long as one or both have acceptable alternatives other than dealing with each other. If they can go elsewhere to satisfy their needs, no solution is possible. If, however, either or both must somehow come to agreement, there is a chance that they can enter into a genuine problem-solving effort.

Beyond the problem of inaccuracies in communication, then, lies the need to resolve genuine differences of value, point of view, and personal preference. The resolution of such differences requires that communication be exact and precise, but it also requires that these differences be explored frankly. The important thing is to find common ground. The manager and employee who differ about how a job ought to be done should at least agree on what must be accomplished to meet the organization's objectives. The husband and wife who disagree about how to discipline a child must at least agree on the need for raising a child who is socially and intellectually competent. Friends who cannot decide which golf course is best must at least agree that playing with one another is quite as important a source of pleasure as the course.

When real differences of value preference exist, the beginning of problem solution is the realization that the problem is never solved just because one person can successfully impose his choice on the other. If the other can escape from such an arrangement, he will! There must be something more substantial than mere domination of the relationship if problem solving is to occur.

## An Interpersonal Problem-Solving Discipline

With this foundation, we can now lay down a procedure for interpersonal problem solving in cases where both parties want to find a solution.

1. *Build a feedback loop immediately.* Unless you have some way of finding out how your messages are being understood, and unless you are sure you understand the messages you are receiving, you may find yourself forever lost in a semantic wasteland. You will never *find* the problem, much less solve it.

2. *Start with simple messages.* You need not stoop to the pre-school level of communicating, but you should at least be sure that the words you use are reliable in that they are commonly understood. The earliest messages transmitted should be those that have the greatest likelihood of being interpreted accurately.

3. *Insure that each message is received with 100 percent reliability.* Before proceeding from one message to the next, it is essential that the first message be verified. As long as errors of understanding occur and remain uncorrected, any effort toward problem solution is doomed to failure.

4. *Define the problem to the satisfaction of both parties.* You must keep working until you find the real differences, if any, which separate you.

5. *Explore a full range of alternative solutions.* If you are out merely to impose your views, this is the point at which things will go sour. You will be so busy forcing your point of view that you will not have time to look for alternatives. If, however, you are willing to seek solutions to your problem beyond those you have previously considered, you will now be able to move toward agreement. It is essential at this stage that evaluation of solutions be deferred, except for purposes of comparing them with your definition of the problem to see how well they fit it. More and more alternatives must be sought until all the possibilities have been exhausted. Typically, the exploration stage, if both sides conduct themselves unselfishly, is the one at which the problem may begin to solve itself.

6. *Rank solutions from better to poorer and agree upon the best.* In the end, most of the proposals will be easy to judge; but, if they are not, you may need to go back, redefine the problem, and re-evaluate the solutions arrived at in terms of their efficacy in dealing with it.

These steps in an interpersonal problem-solving discipline are listed in Exhibit 7. When they fail, most frequently it is because fear, distrust, and pride get in the way. However, as long as there is commitment to the maintenance of the relationship, these emotions can be overcome by simple adherence to the procedure outlined. The six

# EXHIBIT 7

## Problem-Solving Discipline

---

Build a communication feedback loop immediately.

Start with simple messages.

Insure that each message is received with 100 percent reliability before proceeding on to the next.

Define the problem to the satisfaction of both sender and receiver.

Explore a full range of alternative solutions.

Rank solutions from better to poorer; agree upon and implement the best solution.

---

steps provide a way of depersonalizing the problem and making it easier to solve by stripping it down to its essential elements. The real stumbling block is encountered when either or both parties are so involved in individually conceived solutions that they cannot stop and listen to any opposing points of view.

# PART THREE

---

*The Organization as Communicator*

# 9

———————•◆•———————

# *Climate Setting:*

# *The Establishment of Values*

THE EXISTENCE of an industry devoted to influencing American tastes and needs through advertising, the prevalence of public-address systems in plants and offices, the persistent efforts to censor or restrict forms of communication which are feared to have an adverse influence upon some segments of our society, the popular belief in the efficacy and power of "brainwashing"—all point to one inescapable conclusion: People can be motivated, directed, or influenced by communication. It has been suggested that advertising is essential to maintaining the American economy at its present high level. This theory—while perhaps easy to refute with respect to a specific product—is difficult to reject in general. The constant flood of information directed at the public through advertising attests to its significance as a method of focusing interest and attention on material possessions. The aims, goals, and purposes of the economic community take precedence in our culture. Most of us are convinced that our personal worth can be measured and demonstrated by the quantity and variety of the goods we have accumulated.

## What Price Persuasion?

Despite all this, it has been conjectured that even the most massive advertising campaign for a specific product probably does not influence more than 1 to 4 percent of the population to alter its preferences with respect to acceptance or purchases.* One typical study investigated the influence of an intensive campaign to sell U.S. Savings Bonds. Every element of the advertising and promotional art had been brought to bear in the attempt to persuade people to buy the bonds. On analysis, however, it was found that the net result was to elicit new pledges from no more than 4 percent of the total audience.

There are two ways of looking at this result. In relative terms, such a percentage seems rather trivial; we would expect the best efforts of advertising to have more effect if it is to pay its way in our economy. On the other hand, 1 or 2 percent of all the sales of soap, automobiles, or even savings bonds still represents a tremendous amount in gross sales. In 1965, for example, 1 percent of the cigarette market equaled $60 million in sales.

In the political arena, a shift of 1 or 2 percent of the voters can mean the difference between victory and defeat in many elections. When candidate preferences are closely balanced—as they often are in a two-party system—opponents battle fiercely for the favor of that small segment of the electorate that controls the outcome.

Beyond the desire to influence buyers or voters lie deeper issues which are not often noticed. Yet promulgation and acceptance of these issues through public communication may be at least as important as the shift in sales or voter preference which is the direct and obvious subject of advertising. The massive and intensive bond drives of World War II were a particularly effective way of focusing public attention on the problems of financing the nation's military effort. They also served to shore up a popular ethic of personal self-sacrifice

---

* "The Obstinate Audience," *The American Psychologist*, May 1964.

in support of total war. Product shortages, personal inconveniences, higher taxes—these were made more palatable by a continuing appeal for still greater exertions in behalf of the national good as a logical and important component of the government's campaign for public backing.

In the same way, what often seems an inordinate emphasis on soap in present-day advertising is perhaps a means of focusing public attention on the values of personal cleanliness and hygiene. To be sure, the promotional gimmicks in current favor may change the specific preferences of relatively few purchasers—but that change will no doubt pay for the advertising and, for what it may be worth, maintain the high consumption of various hygienic products throughout the economy.

As to political campaigning, the candidates and their partisans may succeed in changing only a small percentage of the votes, but the campaigning process itself focuses attention on the importance of government in every individual's life. It is often decried that nearly one-third of our citizens do not participate in any given presidential election and that as many as one-half to two-thirds do not become involved in state and local elections. Yet it is noteworthy that two-thirds of the voters do go to the polls in a "presidential year" and that as many as half do concern themselves with state and local elections. Added to this is the fact that the two-party process is often so successful at balancing the attractions and drawbacks of opposing candidates that many voters cannot make a choice and therefore do not cast a vote; hence it becomes evident that a significant percentage of those who seem to lack involvement are in fact actively avoiding or withdrawing from the contest. A clash between political personalities may have a powerful impact on these people even though they do not vote, so that, in reality, the involvement of Americans in their government is quite high.

Apparently, therefore, advertising does influence people in our society, though on a relatively smaller scale than we might be inclined to predict offhand. Not only does it sell products and services—or political candidates—but it also highlights attendant questions of importance that are never spelled out. Further, what we see as an inability to influence may, as often as not, be an ability to discourage people from taking action rather than a failure to overcome their lack of interest.

## The Businessman's Ambivalence

What does this mean to the typical business concern, which, in nearly all its activities, reflects its preoccupation with economic and material values? Most Americans, being similarly preoccupied, should be more than willing to go along with its goals and activities; after all, the advertising industry probably does much more to influence them in this direction than it does to promote preferences for specific products. This being the case, it would seem a relatively easy matter to persuade people to support the best interests of the business organization. Why, then, is there so much rebelliousness, recalcitrance, dishonesty, or just plain apathy?

The answer to this question has already been suggested: The problem is one of active withdrawal from the principal goals and purposes of the organization owing to the inability of some people to choose among the alternatives available to them. Frequently, the choice given to employees is an impossible one, just as many political choices are impossible to voters. For example:

> ✧ We exhort employees to become involved in making the business a success by giving unstinted effort to the job. At the same time, we publish strict rules regarding misappropriation of company property or money, and we severely discipline any employee who removes tools, materials, or supplies from the premises without authorization. In effect, we ask for involvement in the success of the organization while we practice and enforce policies which make clear our belief that employees cannot be trusted to put the interests of the company ahead of their own selfish interests. There is a sharp discrepancy between what we say to employees and what we do to them, and this discrepancy is, of course, obvious. (Perhaps the rule of two outlined earlier derives from the fact that our words are so often at odds with our actions that some degree of consonance between them is necessary before our words can become believable.)
>
> ✧ We call for a high level of individual initiative, responsibility, and self-direction—without error. A man who takes an unusual or unconventional course of action is likely to be

criticized for it whether or not he is successful. We tolerate mistakes only when they can be blamed on someone else. Again, the discrepancy between what we ask of people and what we permit them to do clearly belies our words.

✧ We call for high-quality craftsmanship and performance, but we do nothing about the supervisor who carelessly issues incomplete or inaccurate instructions or the engineer who creates designs that can't be followed in manufacture.

Thus there is a prevalent tendency in business to talk from a basis of lofty ideals and principles while we act from a solid foundation of skepticism, distrust, and disrespect for the abilities and rights of customers and employees. Small wonder that our efforts at influencing, informing, directing, and motivating often fall flat.

## Getting People to Use Their Heads

Recently, a manager asked a consulting firm whether it could suggest some way to get people in his organization to take more initiative and come up with more innovations. His operation involved the production and maintenance of highly complex electronic equipment used by the government. It offered a great many opportunities for making errors, but there also were many opportunities to identify better ways of assembling and, occasionally, simplifying the equipment. Even the most highly qualified technical engineering and designing team could not be expected to have all the answers; the employees were clearly in the best possible position both to pinpoint errors and to suggest improvements. The employees, however, seemed entirely unwilling to concern themselves with either. As a result, major mistakes continued to be made in the production of the equipment, and innovations were so rare as to be virtually nonexistent.

As the situation was being discussed, a general foreman came into the manager's office with a major problem: "That new guy, Ben, who was promoted to receiving expediter last week, just stacked up 300 cases of parts in the middle of the floor in the 72-B production area. I'm going to have to pull all my people off their regular jobs to get the stuff out of the way so we can keep on working."

The manager was visibly disturbed by this announcement. "Why did he do that? He ought to know that you can't handle all those parts in your area at once."

"Well, he *says* it's because I told him they all had to be delivered by this date, but anybody ought to know that doesn't mean we want them in the middle of the floor. I won't be able to use most of them for a couple of months."

"O.K. I'll get Harry over in Shipping and Receiving to put somebody else on the job. Ben obviously doesn't have the stuff. . . . By the way, that Steve Snider in your operation who worked all last weekend to get the L-14 order did a terrific job, didn't he?"

"He certainly did. I put a letter of commendation in his file."

"Do you think we ought to do anything more for him?"

"No, all Steve needs is a pat on the back from time to time to keep him going. He's pretty well satisfied with what he has."

At this point, the consultant could contain himself no longer. "How can you be so sure that this fellow Steve Snider is willing to settle for a pat on the back for doing an outstanding job?"

The general foreman was startled; for a moment he looked at the manager as though to ask, "Who's this guy?" Then he turned to the consultant: "Steve's a good man. He always does a job the way you want it. He's just satisfied, that's all. He's one of the few people I've got who's really earning his salary. Every chance I get, I tell him what a good job he's doing and how much better he is than anybody else in my outfit. You ought to see him—he eats it up!"

"But how do you know he doesn't expect a lot more from you in the long run?"

The foreman answered testily, "I just know. I'm in touch with my people, and I can tell what they think."

"I guess that's as good a reason as any," said the manager. "Thanks for keeping me informed, Harry. I'll take care of that receiving expediter for you."

When the foreman had left, the consultant continued to worry. "I still can't see what reason you all have for assuming that the back-slapping routine is all a good man needs. It seems to me that Steve Snider deserves an awful lot more."

The manager responded with great deliberation: "Well, I've heard that Steve is doing some agitating, trying to bring a union into the plant. And I'm not so sure we want to do anything special for someone who's a troublemaker. O.K., he's been a good producer, and we were figuring he'd be a candidate for promotion if a chance came along. But then I began to hear that he was spending his spare time at the union hall talking to one of the organizers. So now you can bet your boots I think a pat on the back is enough for Steve Snider—maybe even too much for him!"

"And how about that shipping expediter? Do you really plan to replace him because he followed instructions to the letter?"

The manager seemed surprised that the question should even come up. "Of course I intend to remove him! I said I would, and I keep my word! I'm a man of integrity—I do what I say I'll do!"

The consultant realized that he had begun to irritate his potential client. "I certainly didn't mean to imply that you weren't a man of integrity," he apologized, "but it surprised me that you'd take such strong action against an employee who seemed to be doing what he was supposed to do. A few minutes ago you asked me how to get your employees more deeply involved in avoiding unnecessary errors and finding better ways to make your product. Now, when a receiving expediter delivers something he was asked to deliver on the date he was asked to deliver it, even if it isn't needed, isn't he trying to point out that there's a lack of integrity in the way you go about doing business that makes his job difficult, if not impossible?"

"I'm not sure you're the man for this job." The manager's annoyance was evident. "You don't seem to be able to grasp the situation at all. Everybody knows you don't stack 300 cases of parts in the middle of a production area when they won't be used for the next three months. We can't afford to let people do stupid things like that. We have to make it clear that they've got to think about what they're doing. They've got to use their heads. That's what I've been talking to you about—how do we get people to use their heads?"

*Unwillingness to See the Whole Problem*

The consultant realized that his sale was lost and that all he could do was to see that he and the manager parted without ill feelings. He chose his words carefully.

"It's been my observation that people use their heads pretty well. At least, they use their brains to take care of their most essential needs. Which of those needs come to the forefront depends on how people are handled in the organization. If it's most important for a person to keep his nose clean and avoid mistakes, all the brainpower he's got will be put to work in doing just that. I know you're a man of integrity and will keep your word now that you've given it, but it seems to me that removing the expediter will advertise your unwillingness to tolerate out-of-the-ordinary action by your employees and make them careful to avoid any innovation. Furthermore, removing a man for carrying out orders may be the best way in the world to get a union in here; it may be proof positive to your employees that they can't protect themselves from arbitrary discipline and that they need the union to do it for them. Is keeping your word with a general foreman that essential? Wouldn't it be better to call him back and discuss the matter further?"

"You bright college fellows with the fancy degrees can certainly twist things around," said the manager, "so an ordinary guy like me has trouble knowing whether he's doing the right thing or not." Then his voice took on a solemn note. "You may even have a point there, but I still feel I should stick to my word. And if people want to use that as an excuse for trying to get a union in here, we'll just see what happens. I've given my word that no union is going to get a foothold in this organization if I have anything to say about it, and I'm going to keep my word on that, too."

"I'm certain you will." The discussion continued for another few minutes as the consultant attempted to soothe the manager's bruised ego. Then he took his leave.

On the way back to his office, the consultant dictated his report. Having covered the substance of the discussion, he summarized as follows:

> There appears to be no possibility of establishing a consulting relationship with this manager at the present time. He is not willing to look at a problem in all its complexity and deal with more than one or two pieces of it at a time. He would undoubtedly expect much more from us than we could deliver because of his inability to see the difficulties that he himself is creating. It is clear that he resorts to harsh penalties to discourage mistakes—even mistakes that are technically not the responsibility of the employees who make them. On the other hand, it is equally clear that he does not reward the really outstanding producers. We may reasonably expect the workforce at this plant to devote most of its time to avoiding

being penalized; little or no effort will go toward achieving exceptional or even good performance. In addition, it seems altogether likely that there will be strong pressures from employees to obtain union representation as a result of their need to protect themselves from arbitrary punishment.

Under these circumstances, there is little we could do to help, and taking on this assignment might well be courting failure. We should, therefore, not pursue this particular contract any further.

## Integrity Not Enough

Had this consultant not been relatively new to the game, he would not have antagonized his potential client and had to undo the damage as best he could. He might even have found a way to communicate with the manager and salvage the contract. However, he did learn a great deal from this experience about the way in which the employer-employee relationship in many organizations actually works.

To the extent that managers are conscious of any connection between what they say and what they do, they work hard to maintain a reasonable consistency and even take long risks to keep from jeopardizing their own sense of integrity. But, too often, they are unaware that they talk on an idealistic level and act on a realistic one. The result is that their communication—in this case, exhortations for error-free performance and productive innovation—is totally at odds with their action. If this manager really wanted innovation or exceptional performance, he would avoid discouraging his employees by such action as removing the receiving expediter. Further, he would take steps to insure that standout performers are rewarded early and adequately. Instead, what happens? Penalties are assessed quickly, and rewards are given slowly and cautiously.

Communication within a business organization not only fails in many cases to influence the 1 or 2 percent reached by good advertising and promotion, it also may result in establishing a set of values directly opposed to those sought. Management calls for greater initiative and responsibility, only to see less being exercised—it is almost as though the employees have heard the request but have deliberately chosen to be obstructive. This is precisely what does often happen when communication is out of phase with action. Employees recognize the discrepancy; and, because they would like to use more initiative and take more responsibility, they register a protest. That is why efforts to direct or motivate which are inappropriate to the climate of the organization are more likely to have negative than positive results, so that some managers feel they are better off not to communicate with employees at all.

In assessing and developing a company communication program, therefore, it is critical to remember this principle: When communication with employees is out of phase with the actual, day-to-day practices of the organization, it is in danger of backfiring. Of course, a manager must be a man of integrity in that he keeps his word, but such integrity is the easiest kind in the world to practice (often at the expense of the organization). What is essential is that communication be consistent with practice and that this consistency be plain and obvious for all to see.

## Communicative Activities Within the Organization

Once again, let us look at possible ways of applying some of the principles we have propounded.

*The company newspaper.* Read a house organ produced by any company and ask yourself: To what extent does this publication really discuss critical issues—level of profitability, success in meeting the needs of the market place competition, achivement of business goals, and the like? To what extent does management express its philosophy effectively? What percentage of the columns is filled with trivia? Have company or department failures ever been discussed candidly?

For the most part, a house organ is a pretty superficial communication device. Probably it never really faces critical issues, such as the removal and replacement of managers or a change in product scope. Perhaps there are good reasons for not discussing such sensitive matters in print, but these more than any others receive wide coverage in the company's rumor mill—most of it informal, inaccurate, and over-the-back-fence communication.

What is ludicrous about this state of affairs is that a manager or employee is typically removed because he has been judged ineffective and an example needs to be set for others as to what constitutes ineffective behavior. Yet nothing is ever said about the lessons to be drawn from the incident—except by way of the grapevine—and the reasons for disciplinary or corrective action are never made explicit. Similarly, when we change product lines to keep the organization healthy, we leave the employees to guess why. Strange though it may seem, the underlying message of the typical house organ is *management's unwillingness to communicate with its employees about issues of genuine importance.*

It may be, of course, that no particular harm is done or even that positive benefit is achieved by pursuing such policy. A highly competitive company that wants to keep its rivals in the dark may very well be justified in withholding from employees any information that might be "leaked." For the rest, however, such a policy would seem to be consonant with communication practices based on a preference for employee apathy. It would be unrealistic only if higher management began to pontificate about open, free communication between employees and managers without enforcing that policy. Management, in fact, can expect trouble whenever it uses high ideals to justify its point of view while it continues to use "the facts of business life" as the basis of its action.

Naturally this works both ways. When the uncommunicative management learns that its employees are organizing and electing union representatives, it may—and generally does—charge that they have not been open and aboveboard about vital issues. But management should not be surprised if the employees seem cynical.

To the extent that the house organ is in tune with the climate of the organization, no one can complain much. The autocratic manager who keeps his own counsel and limits the sheet to a pleasant, sterile medium for the discussion of personalities or the publication of want ads is at least being honest with himself and his employees. On the other hand, the modern, permissive manager who genuinely seeks full employee involvement must be prepared to use his house organ as an open line of communication. If he fails to include significant information in it, the message his employees read into that failure is, "I don't trust you enough to be completely candid with you." And he can expect employees to be no less cautious in communicating with him.

The important rules for successful publication of a house organ are the following:

1. Assess the relationship between actual practices and communication in the organization.
2. Determine the real needs of the organization and set goals to satisfy those needs.
3. If there is a discrepancy between actual practices and communication, determine what change is necessary and call on the house organ to support that change. In all likelihood, the house organ will never do its job properly when practices do not change as management values change.
4. Use the principles of effective promotion and advertising for all they are worth as long as communication and management practices are in agreement. In this situation, the communicator can make the greatest impact, the best reputation for himself, and the most profitable contribution to the enterprise.

*Other written communication.* Public speaking and effective report writing have always been popular subjects for reading and personal study by businessmen. When either course is offered as part of an educational program, there are always more students than the instructor can handle. This is perhaps a natural concomitant of the awe in which we hold words throughout our culture. However, it also reflects a recognition that the average person, in spite of 12 or more years' schooling, is aware of his ineptitude in both written and spoken communication.

This is painfully true with respect to the written word. Much written communication is, in fact, so poor that it cannot be understood. It is loaded with ambiguity, it is based on incorrect information, or it lacks essential points.

Too many people look on writing as a chore. When they sit down to write, they scribble away as fast as they can; and when they are "finished," they can barely wait to get rid of the results. They do not review, reread, or rewrite what they have set down on paper. They have not yet learned that everyone who writes finds himself in blind alleys in the construction of sentences and phrases or the exposition of complex ideas; that, to break out of those blind alleys, they must often go back and make a new start. They are somewhat like the hiker who is intent on taking a short cut even though he must surmount so many obstacles in the course of it that he reaches his destination much later than he would if he had taken what seemed to be the roundabout route.

The fact is that writing, like every other effort of any consequence, demands our best efforts if it is to be of high quality. This means that we must

- ✧ Think out what we have to say.
- ✧ Be certain we have something worthwhile to say before we start; that is, have an objective.
- ✧ Dictate or write with our objective clearly in mind.
- ✧ Carefully reread what we have written to see whether we have achieved our objective; rewrite as necessary.
- ✧ Have others read and criticize the results when the message contained is important.
- ✧ Be willing to admit that no one can ever be a perfect communicator.
- ✧ Be willing to assess, specifically and energetically, the accuracy with which the communication is received.

Obviously it is a good idea, with written messages as much as with oral man/manager communication, to monitor the messages we send out and build feedback loops to assess the reliability of their reception. Most problems of written communication, however, stem from

1. A lack of concern about the message's reception and the extent to which it is understood.
2. The assumption that a message will be entirely clear to the reader because it is clear to the writer.

*Insuring Accuracy*

We stated in an earlier chapter that one of the fringe benefits of the widespread use of data processing in industry may be that eventually most managers will have to learn how to use computers. In the process, they will undoubtedly come to realize that there may be an error in a communication even when every effort has been made to insure accuracy. We can give instructions to people in a variety of forms, permitting them to make comparisons and so verify our intentions, but communication with a computer in the form of program instructions or data must be precise. There is no other way to get the computer to respond accurately; it has no capacity for dealing with varied instructions except to the extent that errors are anticipated in the original program. A single oversight may invalidate weeks of work.

The computer programmer knows the need for building a feedback loop immediately. He puts into his program a standard problem, one whose answer is known, and tests directly to determine whether the computer will provide the expected answer. If his test is valid, no question remains as to accuracy of his instructions. In written communication, on the other hand, we are inclined to overlook the opportunity for checking the accuracy with which our messages are received, and we fail to compensate for the many small errors that so easily creep in.

One way to get around this is to use repetition freely. Many written messages are sparse and uninformative in draft form. Only as they are expanded do they begin to take on substance. Their intent and meaning are most likely to be clear when the communicator has repeated his message once and perhaps even several times in the course of writing. This does not mean that the same words should be used again and again. Instead, the message should be rephrased so as to add variety and color. Comparing each new statement with the previous ones, the recipient can extract the common, consistent thread running through them. In other words, he can form a hypothesis about the first message and test it against the second, the third, and so on.

The problem with this kind of writing, of course, is that it can become excessively wordy. The perfectionist who is concerned with reducing to a minimum the chance of being misunderstood can keep on writing forever, and this is precisely the criticism most often leveled at business writing. In the effort to correct it, we find ourselves trapped between our concern for making our message reliable and our need to insure that it will not be so long or so verbose as to put the reader to sleep. Finding the optimum balance is clearly a matter of individual judgment; few useful rules can be laid down. The writer can err in the direction either of overterseness or of over-verbosity, but varying his style appropriately should, with practice, help to maintain a desirable balance.

## Feedback from Higher Management

The writer who has doubts about the quality of his writing should obtain a candid evaluation of it. He may, however, have difficulty getting an honest opinion (which may account for the popularity of many report-writing courses). This is particularly true if he is a highly placed manager who spends a good part of his day sending written messages down to subordinates. "What kind of double-talk is it this time?" they may consider aloud, but he is unlikely to hear such remarks. Especially in organizations where mistakes are heavily penalized, subordinates are typically fearful of not being able to understand what their manager wants of them. When they receive ambiguous messages, they find it easier not to act at all or to take some standard course of action which will not involve personal risk.

Most upward communication in this kind of organization is excessively labored. Indeed, one of the most useful measures of a punitive climate is the amount of time, energy, and sweat that goes into a written report which must be sent to higher management. If the best efforts of all the employees involved are directed toward perfecting upward communication, while only the most superficial efforts go into the downward variety, chances are that people feel they must avoid criticism at all costs.

This is an unfortunate situation, since the boss—being free to speak his mind openly—could be an excellent source of useful feedback about the effectiveness of a subordinate's ordinary, everyday messages. To benefit from his criticism, however, the employee would have to communicate with his superior in a normal way, and few are able to do this. Perhaps it is unrealistic to expect anything else, since criticism of whatever kind from higher management is assumed (often with good reason) to color all other evaluations of the employee's performance. Where—to emphasize the point once more —it is essential to avoid all forms of failure, *real learning is impossible.*

Turn the situation around, though: Create a climate in which mistakes are not only tolerated but used as opportunities for higher management to support and coach employees in more effective performance. Then communication can be improved readily by means of two simple expedients: (1) Require that all messages be brief; (2) evaluate the effectiveness of all upward communication in terms of clarity and utility.

### The Double-Talk Syndrome

Regrettably, what is more likely to develop is double-talk. Lengthy reports which say nothing, or which reach contradictory conclusions so as to satisfy everyone and offend no one, are the most common. Every effort is exerted to make them look impressive and show the extensive time, effort, and concern that have gone into their preparation.

The message in such reports is clear: The employees are knocking themselves out to please the boss, knowing full well that his reaction to this ploy will be to withhold criticism. Yet criticize he must. As long as managers accept reports that reveal a need to be deferential, respectful, and fearful of higher authority rather than clear and informative, double-talk communication will prevail.

### For a Change of Climate

The tough, results-oriented manager who demands cogent, meaningful communication may, of course, get no reports at all, or he may get them too late to take action. This is in line with the central fact of formal organizational communication which we have cited continually: People who are afraid of failing will direct their energies toward the avoidance of failure.

The average organization, on the other hand, can improve its internal communication markedly and almost immediately by

1. Initiating a course in effective writing, to be taken by all managers and employees who are required to submit reports.
2. Placing a moratorium on penalties for poor reports.

3. Discussing reports from subordinates openly and candidly; coaching them in how to improve their writing skills.
4. Taking particular care to transmit only clear, easily understood reports and instructions to employees.

Almost every kind of written communication—letters, memos, policy statements, job descriptions, product specifications, business objectives, performance standards—can be expected to benefit from this concerted approach.

# 10

---◆◆●---

# *Monitoring Upward Communication:*
# *Feedback Completed*

BUSINESS ORGANIZATIONS are designed to insure that downward communication is heard and attended to. In the process, upward communication is at best muted. As a result, important messages from employees to management are often in code—that is, their real intent is disguised.

The employee whose principal concern is the timing of his next salary increase will rarely ask, "When am I going to get a raise?" If increases have been associated with performance appraisals, this employee is much more likely to say, "Appraisals don't come on time around here." On the surface, it would seem that improvement is needed in the scheduling of performance reviews. In fact, however, more frequent appraisals without corresponding discussions of salary may be an even greater disappointment to this employee; he will discover that he has to endure negative judgments from his manager without the offsetting pleasure of hearing about a salary increase in the end.

Much the same is true of all employee complaints and grievances. The typical employee, when he has a complaint to register, first casts around to find one that will be acceptable to his manager. The real grievance is hidden behind the mask of this standard, acceptable "gripe." In this fashion, employees can express their concern with a minimum of risk to themselves. In the decoding process, moreover, it is altogether too likely that the manager will interpret the grievance in terms of his own perspectives and miss the real message entirely.

Higher management, therefore, needs a feedback loop of its own. It is not enough to assume that problems are bound to come to light. In hierarchical organizations, problems tend to be kept hidden until they have festered so long and become so severe that they are ready to erupt in conflict and violent confrontation.

## What Management Can Do

Several courses of action are open to the management that wants to establish a feedback loop for upward communication from employees:

1. Staff people may serve this purpose. These people—specialists without direct authority over production or employees —can observe what is going on and often hear employee complaints in raw, undisguised form—especially if they are known to be helpful, discreet, and not inclined to preach. This is not so strange as it might seem. Employees have quite as much at stake in being understood by management as management has in being understood by employees. Given an opportunity to talk openly in a situation where he need not be afraid of punishment, the average employee will be quite candid. When, however, staff people are overly concerned about their authority or status and devote a large share of their time to proving their importance, they are likely to be looked on as interlopers and spies. Then they will get no information at all from employees.

2. An outside consultant may be brought in to serve the same

purpose. Indeed, the principal role of the consulting firm may be that of an outsider who has nothing at stake in the internal power struggles and can receive confidences with a fair degree of safety. Of course, the consultant first has to prove his honesty and reliability and demonstrate his willingness to protect his sources of information. If he is able to convince people that he can be trusted with the truth, he will probably hear it.

3. Management may show its tolerance of employee complaints in a variety of ways, including not only its willingness to hear what employees have to say but even its insistence on being given the straight dope. Sensitivity to employee needs, concerns, and problems alerts a manager to listen more carefully, take more time, probe more deeply to get at the truth. This can work wonders. For instance, employees may be complaining about toolroom privileges, although their real grievance is the severity of the disciplinary action taken against those who enter the toolroom without authorization. If the manager is shrewd enough to know there is something wrong that isn't being brought out, he may, by tactful questioning and close listening, be able to get it into the open where it has a chance of solution.

Faced with a misunderstanding or other failure of communication with its employees, management too often adopts a defensive posture, insisting that what it thinks is right and what the employees think must therefore be wrong. This tactic is routinely tried by motorists with policemen, by husbands with wives, and by parents with children. We should have learned by now that it is a relatively ineffective technique for getting one's own way and a sure method of stalling progress in communication.

To a large extent, therefore, the most important factor in improving upward communication from employees to management is to avoid this defensive attitude. The manager who can deal with complaints confidently and without fear, and who can encourage the complete exploration of a problem even when it concerns him directly, will be able to get the fullest information about what is really happening in his organization.

## Communication and Discipline

A peculiar role in this picture of upward communication is played by discipline. Essential to any organization, discipline sets the limits of permissible behavior; it tells employees how far they can go—what they can and cannot do.

Take the average plant employee, for example. He must be shown how to avoid injury on his job. An industrial plant is no place to take risks with life or property; therefore, any behavior that might jeopardize safety must be dealt with immediately—as when workers are found smoking, against company rules, near materials which can catch fire or explode.

Discipline also is involved in utilizing the efforts and assets of the enterprise to achieve realistic and attainable goals. Organizational capabilities are limited, and they should be carefully applied to a range of objectives which will employ them fruitfully without overextending and destroying them. As a case in point, it would be foolish for a small organization that is experienced in the manufacture of small plastic products to undertake large metal parts. Most decisions, however, are much less obvious than this, and they require a high degree of management experience, skill, and judgment. And the overall job of coordinating the company's full activity and resources toward the chosen ends requires the use of rewards and penalties.

## Top Management's Responsibility

Most typically, it is the top of the organization that provides the coordination and determines the rewards and penalties. The manager most likely to be removed if goals are not met is the one who has failed to apply himself, who is unwilling to accept the limitations placed on him by higher management, or who has goals antithetical to those of the organization. Similarly vulnerable, however, is the maverick at the top who will not work as a member of the team and so is potentially destructive to the achievement of organizational objectives or even to the company's survival.

In a large corporation, whenever there is a significant change in management personnel there is likely to be a change in the style of management. Suppose an executive who has a free-wheeling style and gives his subordinates a substantial amount of autonomy is replaced by one who keeps tight control and insists on reviewing every decision of consequence. Employees—be they managers, workers, or whatever—who resist this change in style are playing a game of "bet your career." If they cannot adapt to the new style, they have the choice of quitting or waiting until they are removed.

In casual, informal conversations these questions are asked and answered: Can you get along with the new manager? Can you communicate with him? Can you cooperate with him? From now on, the rules of the organization may be completely different; people who continue to operate under the old ones must be weeded out or isolated; those who accept the new regime become the bright stars on the company horizon.

Discipline at this level is not so much a matter of meting out punishment as it is a matter of knowing whether communication with subordinates is possible. It is a matter of rewarding those managers who can achieve openness and confidence and eliminating those who reflect suspicion and lack of candor. Discipline and communication thus are closely related.

## At Lower Levels

Lower down in the organization, discipline takes somewhat different forms, although the results may be the same. At these levels, the employee who fights the system and is unwilling or unable to adjust to it is disciplined unceremoniously.

The soldier who fails to keep in step, to get out of bed at reveille, to respond properly to orders, or to conform to military custom may eventually face court-martial. The student who fails to attend class or earn acceptable grades is dropped from school. The service club member who fails to pay his dues or contribute to the club's activities is encouraged to resign. Just so, the employee who fails to follow orders from his supervisor is subject to disciplinary action ranging from a mild reprimand to dismissal without notice.

Every organization has central values and concerns toward which it bends its efforts. Other values and concerns are clearly excluded because the organization considers them antithetical or even dangerous. Employees who do not contribute to the stated goals or who indulge in forbidden activities must be brought into line or removed.

It is the negative goals, the taboos, which generally elicit the strongest reactions from management in the way of discipline. Almost every organization, for example, has a rule against diverting its assets or resources to "unauthorized personal use." The employee who turns in a forged billing to support an expense account, steals tools or materials, uses machinery after hours, or spends excessive work time in personal activities must suffer the penalty. What the employee is to be paid for his productive efforts—salary, benefits, working conditions—is spelled out by the employer in advance, and any attempt by the employee to redefine or expand the terms of his employment without the employer's consent is intolerable.

The material resources of this world are limited, and it is only sensible to restrain people from simply taking whatever they want. Without restraints there would be no order in society. Similarly, without restraints a business could not survive. Rules are essential, therefore, and must be enforced. What is unfortunate about discipline in this area is that so much of the organization's activity is spent on such matters.

Discipline should be positive; it should not be limited to taboos. Overconcentration on taboos at the expense of positive accomplishment may even encourage defiance of the rules; for, if employees believe the organization seeks to take advantage of them, they may feel that they have every right to try to outwit management. It would be a good deal more constructive to protect organizational assets directly, rather than through threat of punishment, and link disciplinary action with failure to support established goals.

In the rigidly hierarchical organization, this approach is not entirely practical because, as we have seen, employees at the lowest levels have no choice as to what they do. Their jobs are spelled out and must be done exactly as defined. It is only in the upper reaches of the organization that employees have any choice as to how they go about doing their jobs and the question of concurrence in goals and objectives can become a critical issue.

## Discipline Without Awareness

A basic problem with discipline, as it is often applied, is that it is enforced without full awareness of its purpose. If, as suggested, discipline is a way of coordinating the efforts and assets of the organization toward achievement of specific objectives as well as a way of discouraging activity antithetical to those goals, then it follows that discipline should be used only in fairly clear-cut cases and with the conscious intention of demonstrating what is and is not acceptable.

More often, management takes disciplinary action when it feels it has been pushed to the wall and can no longer tolerate infraction of the rules. It then administers its penalties with a vague sense of guilt. Discipline is too frequently justified on moral rather than on sound business grounds.

The problem in some organizations may be rooted in the lack of well-conceived objectives and goals. The manager is vague as to his future activities; he keeps his own counsel in all respects, taking sudden and dramatic advantage of opportunities, as they arise, even at the expense of missing better ones because his employees are not involved in the decision-making process. He is continually changing the rules to fit changing conditions (which actually is rather realistic), but he seldom articulates the rule changes except by disapproval of conduct which was previously acceptable or by an unexpected reward for behavior which was formerly penalized or regarded with indifference.

## The Autocrat

Under an autocratic manager of this type, downward communication of goals and objectives is carried out like a game of charades. Disciplinary action is principally a way of sensitizing employees to sudden shifts in the autocratic manager's preferences and of keeping employees flexible. If the autocrat is a particularly capable man who knows how to deal with his market and his product, this arrangement may be quite effective. He uses disciplinary action to teach his employees to "jump when I say jump."

The analogy to the military is obvious: When the best way to succeed is to let one highly skilled and knowledgeable individual run the whole show, everyone in the organization has to be trained to a high degree of sensitivity to the leader. Rank and file then become extremely capable interpreters of his charades.

There are two specific problems related to this manner of communicating. First, the democratic institutions of our society enable people to decide that they don't want to live in constant fear of autocratic discipline and provide mechanisms for limiting the autocrat's behavior. Employees may propose and support legislation to limit their employer or protect their "rights." They may form a union with which to fight back. Even military servicemen have been successful over the past 50 years in significantly moderating the power which their officers once had over them. And, while these curbs clearly limit the effectiveness of the autocratic style of managing, they do not eliminate the autocrat's right to manage as much as some people might believe.

Second, the autocrat handles the process of managing—that is, applying resources to the production of goods or services which will meet market needs—in a highly subjective fashion. His motives and intentions are not apparent to his employees; his objectives and purposes are hidden and thus not available to employees for use in measuring their own performance. Herein lie the opportunities for communicating more effectively through discipline.

Discipline should be administered impersonally, not punitively. It should serve to demonstrate the seriousness of management's commitment to specific objectives. It should eliminate from the organization people who are unable or unwilling to cooperate in working toward these objectives. Such discipline will be valid and defensible as long as the organization makes a contribution to society; without it, the organization could not survive.

*Supervisory Discipline*

In recent studies by Norman R. F. Maier,* a group of industrial foremen were asked how they would handle certain hypothetical dis-

---

*Personnel Journal*, April 1965.

ciplinary problems, and a group of workers were asked how they would react to the action proposed by the foremen. These studies demonstrated that a subordinate's willingness to abide by the rules is likely to increase when the foreman does not enforce the prescribed penalties.

In the research, one of the rules being violated forbade working on a telephone pole without a safety belt. It was found that employees who were subtly and skillfully made aware of the importance of the rule were far more likely to honor it than those who were merely punished for violating it. The irony here is that it is by breaking a rule himself that the foreman has an opportunity to dramatize the company's humaneness. By failing to take disciplinary action when it is specifically required by the regulations, he gains compliance. In other words, the foreman who stops short of penalizing an infraction of a rule seems to create a genuine appreciation of the purpose back of that rule.

Rules have no purpose or life in themselves. They exist only as adjuncts to the goals and objectives of the organization, and they have meaning only to the extent that they support the achievement of those goals and objectives. This means, more than anything else, that some organizations may need to become more conscious of their objectives. They need to describe in specific terms what they are doing, what they plan to do, and what they should do. Only in this way can discipline be made meaningful, and only then can discipline be carried out in such a way as to encourage and coordinate employee effort toward goal achievement.

Any organization that has been mechanically enforcing the rules should examine its practices to determine just how effectively the written rules support corporate objectives. This examination may even bring to light rules that are downright antithetical to current goals.

## Communicating with the New Employee

Communicating with every new employee begins the first time he walks in the door. The way you handle him tells him immediately what you think of him. Curt, impersonal treatment, excessive delays without apology or explanation, degrading questions on an application blank or in an interview make it plain that you have little respect for him as a person. Warmly courteous, efficient, individualized treatment, on the other hand, communicates your respect and concern. The applicant who is treated disrespectfully may forever despise the company even though he is hired, cheating it whenever he can, whereas the one who discovers that the personnel office is interested in his well-being may forever respect and like the company because it respects and likes him.

Every general manager should occasionally arrange to have a friend go through the employment process in his organization in order to find out what kind of impact it makes. Depending on top management's goals and objectives, that impact may or may not be appropriate. When significant changes in management philosophy take place, the place to implement and reflect those changes most quickly and efficiently may well be the employment office. Unfortunately, this is frequently the last place examined when determining what attitudes new employees form toward the company.

The degree to which the job candidate is informed candidly of opportunities and limitations within the organization, the extent of delay between interview and offer of employment, the manner in which he is placed on the payroll and guided during his first day on the job, the way he is introduced to company procedures, the first impression he gets of his new manager and his fellow employees—all of these may be critical in determining his long-range relationship to the organization and his receptiveness to future communication.

By way of contrast, let's introduce a new employee into the work context in the crudest possible way. When he arrives as a candidate at the employment office, he is kept waiting for several hours. The preliminary interviewer who looks over his application is cool and curt, implying that the applicant's failure to fill in several blanks on the required form is inexcusably stupid. In the course of the interview, the young man is asked some highly personal questions about his relationships with his mother and father and interrogated as to possible illegal or immoral behavior and other equally sensitive matters. He is subjected to a couple of hours of testing whose purpose is not explained to him but is obvious: He has to pass or he doesn't get the job. He is given no hint of the results, and is not even told whether he will ever hear them. In the end he is told, "You'll be hearing from us in a few days," and is sent home without so much as a "Thank you for coming."

Six weeks later, after he has taken a less desirable position, he gets an offer of employment. After some thought, he quits the first job and reports to his new employer. He spends the first day (without pay) undergoing a strict physical examination about which he was told nothing and which he now learns he must pass. Having surmounted this formidable hurdle, he is led in and seated in front of a stony-faced clerk who insists that he sign all kinds of forms that are "absolutely necessary" if he is to be put on the payroll. In other words, he is immediately made aware that a personnel clerk can accept or reject him as an employee, depending on his response to her demands. He may feel that some of the forms are an imposition or are intended to put him at a disadvantage as an employee; but, having already invested so much in the job, he signs them. Finally, he is told to go out into the shop and find the foreman, who points him in the direction of a table or broom or machine and says, "Get to work, Mac!"

Everything that has happened to this young man conveys the unmistakable message, "Look out, buddy, this is a hostile environment. If you aren't careful, you'll be clobbered." The process of sensitizing him to the hazards in his new environment has been carried out effectively and efficiently. The primary lesson the new employee is learning from it all is that his best efforts should be devoted to looking out for his own skin, because the company certainly will not do it for him.

In such a setting, communication between organization and employee is minimal at best. The new employee cannot be expected to worry about the company's interests until he is sure that he no longer has to be preoccupied with his own survival. The organization which really wants the full involvement and cooperation of its employees throughout the total range of its activities would therefore do well to re-evaluate its hiring practices to determine what kinds of relationships they engender. It would be ludicrous for the chief executive of the company who hires employees in this fashion to begin a speech with the words, "The welfare of each employee is our first concern." This would sound so incredible to the newcomer that it would be impossible for him to believe anything that followed.

The matter of orienting the new employee is of equal importance. It is not enough to be kind and gentle in introducing him to his duties and colleagues; some specific effort should be made to advise him about the nature of the organization, its history, its rules and regulations, and its objectives, goals, and purposes. When the new employee is given this opportunity to find out what the organization is all about and realizes he is considered important enough to have time and money spent on him in this way, future communication with him is likely to be successful.

However, it is essential that the orientation session reflect the organization's day-to-day personnel practices. Telling the new employee how concerned management is about his welfare—only to belie that statement the next day—is the surest way to convince him that management cannot be trusted to be truthful. First impressions are important and lasting.

Of course, maybe management doesn't care about its employees and isn't interested in giving them the facts. Maybe management has no intention of being soft and humane, wants people to know their survival is entirely their own affair, and sees fit to warn them in advance what to expect. This is at least an honest and straight-forward definition of the employer/employee relationship, but the employer who adheres to it should expect that his employees will fight back with every method at their disposal. While this sort of arrangement leaves no room for sentimentality or idealism, neither does it offer any opportunity for direct, open communication between employer and employee.

## Communication Between Organization and Environment

It has become fashionable in recent decades to worry about the corporate image. The reason is evident: It is difficult to get along in this world when everyone is afraid of you. Having to ward off periodic attacks from government, competitors, or other interest groups that want to "bell the cat" uses up too much energy that is needed elsewhere. It is a good thing, therefore, for people to see a company as a responsible corporate citizen producing reliable products and services. Once such an image has been successfully achieved, management can go about the business of achieving corporate goals and objectives.

A group of people may not be quite able to achieve common agreement on a positive goal, but it is almost always possible to achieve total commitment to common defense against a feared enemy.

People who might otherwise "keep themselves to themselves" in a rural community may work side by side to chase down the fox that has attacked their chickens. In like fashion, people who usually can't agree on the desirable limits of Congressional power can be readily galvanized into action in support of antibusiness legislation when a corporation is labeled as unscrupulous. Businessmen have found, not only that it pays to stay in close communication with all segments of the external environment, but that it is costly *not* to keep in touch.

In order to achieve a good image, business and industry have had to give up at least one cherished ideal: the right to compete without restraint. The businessman who assumes that it is his right to destroy his competitors or gain absolute control over his market is greatly feared in our society. Anyone who competes so aggressively or so destructively is likely to become the focus of efforts to bring him to heel.

In return for giving up unrestrained competitiveness and becoming a tame tiger, the modern businessman is spared the risk of being himself destroyed in the business jungle. He is therefore able to divert into more productive channels the energies he once devoted to defending himself from the hazards of his environment. The result has been an expansion of productive capacity at a rate heretofore undreamed of. We have discovered that people who don't have to worry about their own survival can put their best efforts into productivity and mutual success. A good reputation in the business community is therefore a positive asset in dealing with government, organized labor, competitors, customers, stockholders, suppliers, and the general public.

The principles of communication we have been discussing apply to all of these. The mere fact that they are outside the organization does not change anything. The creation of a satisfactory company image depends on how effectively management coordinates its self-description with its actions. If they agree, if corporate integrity and beneficence are borne out by both words and actions, the organization will be accepted as a valued contributor to society and allowed to function freely.

In general, messages to customers, stockholders, and the public have one thing in common with messages to employees: Few issues of any real importance are discussed in them. The rule is: Don't hang out any dirty linen in public. Real problems are reserved for discussion in the executive suite and seldom aired in public. For this reason the independent mass media of communication—radio, television, and the press—fill an important liaison role between a business and its external environment. Because these media serve to keep interested groups informed of corporate activities that may not be reported directly in the company's formal communications, stockholders, customers, and the rest trust management more fully than they might if they were limited to the information they receive in official messages.

## How to Fight Rumors

Rumors plague every organization. Embarrassing revelations about new products, policy decisions, and unexpected problems create trouble at every turn. Yet rumors are nothing more than unauthorized, informal news releases about daily events.

Any organization in which issues of real importance are never discussed openly has a well-organized rumor circuit. Most organizational policy decisions and problems are too big to be hidden from view. There is almost always some employee who can be induced to release "confidential" information. Unless management is willing to put time, effort, or money into plugging the obvious leaks, they will continue to feed the rumormongers. However, it may be possible to reduce the scope and influence of the "grapevine" by increasing the amount of information processed through legitimate channels.

Large organizations with effective communication systems often rely on regular staff meetings as their vehicle of communication. Each manager is informed of current happenings; no punches are pulled, and little is withheld. Each is encouraged to discuss the information he has received with his employees. If well conducted, these group meetings in which issues are discussed openly and all their ramifications are explored can be extremely effective. Sometimes they are the best way to enlist the positive support of the employees in preventing embarrassing leaks.

The danger in such leakage is, of course, that facts are readily distorted or even invented by the grapevine. Stories that have no real basis are passed along the circuit together with stories that are true, and no one can tell which is which. Yet the frequent accuracy of the reports makes the grapevine an accepted vehicle of communication in any organization that is stingy with the information its employees need and want. And, when employees lack vital information, informal lines of communication are sometimes used and even manipulated by unscrupulous people, and inaccurate or false information is deliberately passed off as true.

Management must therefore know what information is being bruited about. It is unrealistic to be an ostrich, to pretend the grapevine does not exist. Rather, managers should be aware of it, establish listening points along it, and take appropriate action to reduce the need for it whenever possible. The organization that actively involves its employees in its concerns largely minimizes the scope and impact of rumor.

# 11

---

*The Role of the Group in Communication:*

*Teamwork, Committees, and Task Forces*

"TEAMS ARE ONE THING," said Bill Williams, "but committees are something else again! You know the old saying: A camel is a horse put together by a committee!"

Bill's manager had heard it all before. He knew that, when it came to working on a committee, Bill would just as soon wrestle Indian style. At the same time, he knew that Bill would be among the first to point out the need to have all his employees "playing on the team 100 percent."

In the four and a half years that John Wilson had been Bill's boss, Bill had been consistent in his views; he had never given an inch. On a couple of occasions John had tried to set up task forces designed to carry out committee activities. Bill recognized the subterfuge immediately. "A committee by any other name still smells." This time, however, John had a retort ready: "You know, Bill, of all the animals ever put together, a camel seems to me to be one of the most functional. It may not be much to look at, but a camel is built to do a specific job and does it very well!"

Bill was taken aback. "Well," he muttered, trying to find a quick retort. "You know what I mean, don't you, John? Committees are just no good for getting the job done. Give a man responsibility, authority, and the right people to work for him, and he'll outdo a committee any time."

John was ready for this argument, too: "That may be true, but I can't stop to reorganize and appoint a special manager every time a problem comes up. I need to be able to put together special-purpose teams to handle special problems when they come along. Down at the university they call them 'ad hoc' groups—which means 'for this situation only.' Well, I've got a lot of 'for this situation only' problems, and I need special teams to solve them. Don't get me wrong. A problem that I know you and your people can solve, all by yourselves, you'll get. I wouldn't have it any other way. But, where you have to take into account some of the trickier aspects of marketing, finance, manpower forecasting, and advanced technology—well, admit it, Bill. You and your people can't handle those alone."

"If you'd give me a budget to hire the specialists, I could do a first-class job!"

"Bill, some day maybe you'll get a chance to sit in the top chair in this organization—and if you do you'll discover it isn't so simple. You can't do everything by yourself and keep every detail under your own watchful eye. You have to build an organization that includes people who are competent in the various areas of specialization; and, once you've done that, you don't tear the organization to pieces by playing favorites and letting one man handle some particularly attractive job all by himself. You know perfectly well the rest would blow their stacks if I just gave you carte blanche."

## Facing Up to Realities

Bill was hard put to rebut his boss. But committees simply were no good at all, especially when there was someone around who was good at handling authority, forging a team, and getting results with it. Someone like himself. *He* got results, even if he had to work a 90-hour week in the process. He was a task-oriented tiger; he was good, he knew it, and he wanted to hear his boss say so. He was glad to hear that bit about moving into the top seat, but today he wasn't in a mood to settle for that.

"John," he pleaded, "just give me a chance. I could take over those guys' jobs this minute and do them better than they're being done now. Please—let's not mess around with committees. You know how much I want to make it to the top and how hard I'll work to get there. Let me prove I can handle the job when I get there!"

John was beginning to feel uncomfortable. "Look, Bill, you're a 'do it' man of the first order, and I admit I'd hate having to get along without you. Yes, if we had the time to break you in on every single job here and let you learn it from start to finish, you'd probably do it at least as well as anyone else. But let me put it to you straight: If you had to do each and every job right now, without a chance to learn what they're all about, you'd fall flat on your face."

"Just try me, John." Bill enjoyed nothing better than having an impossible challenge thrown at him. "Put it on the line; let me show you what I can do."

"Hold on, Bill. You may think your energy is a great big bottomless pit, but even you can run out of steam. You can't do everything alone, no matter what you think. You've got to have help, and that help won't come unless you earn it. You can't always buy it, and you can't expect it to be there as a matter of course. You do have a tremendous team going for you right now, simply because your organization isn't so big that you can't keep your finger on every detail of it. You've developed people who are just as competitive and ambitious as you are, and you've given them the kinds of challenges you'd like to have if you were in their shoes. As a result, they respond to you. But let's be realistic: You have to step in every so often and bail a guy out of trouble when he's in over his head, don't you?"

"I sure do. And when a guy caves on me, let me tell you, I don't forget it."

"You don't, I know that, and the guy who asks you for help is never allowed to forget it, either. The last three have all left the company, haven't they?"

"Yeah, I guess they have. But, if you ask me, they really didn't belong here."

"And what did you do, Bill, when you didn't have them to do the work any more?"

"Well, I got other fellows to step in and pick up the pieces, and anything they couldn't do I did myself."

"That's the way you operate, isn't it? You don't ask anybody to do anything you can't do yourself. Right?"

"Right."

"O.K., Bill, what will you do, supposing you're in the top spot, if you put too much pressure on your controller and he walks out? Remember, you're the president. Do you take on the job of controller too?"

"I'd be game to try if it came to that."

"In that case, Bill, I'm not sure the company could afford to have you as president. Your initiative, your drive, your will to win, and your competitive instincts serve you well where you are now. But, if you were on top and you took risks like that, you'd be jeopardizing the entire company to prove you're a superman. Nobody here, including the board of directors, could stand by and let you do it. You have no right to use this company as your personal ante in a great big game of bet-your-career."

John's words were blunt; he made no effort to pull his punches. Bill was a great guy, though he tended to be flamboyant and egotistical. He could get results, and John needed the results Bill got. Bringing matters to a head in this way was not what John had intended. He held his breath, half expecting Bill to take his cue from that hypothetical controller, hand John the job, and walk out. But what John had said was true. If Bill couldn't learn to deal comfortably with his equals in a committee setting, he was riding for a fall.

Bill was a long time in answering. "Are you telling me I've come as far as I'm going to get with this outfit, John?"

"No! I'm telling you that you can go as far as you want to if only you'll face up to the realities of the job. And the first thing you have to learn is how to be a member of a team, a committee, or whatever you want to call it." Bill was a great performer, John went on— unable to back off now—but he was a one-man show. If he couldn't adapt himself to working as part of a team, it was unlikely that John could recommend him for promotion when the day arrived.

## Not Competition but Communication

Bill had never been talked to this way before, and he found he rather enjoyed it. Arguments by the dozen came to mind: "John," he might say, "I don't know what got you off on this committee kick, but I think you'd better look at the facts. A committee is a collection of mealy-mouthed, rubber-spined horse traders. I don't know a textbook anywhere that recommends managing an organization by committee. And what do real top managers say? They won't use committees because they don't trust them!"

But John didn't get where he was on sheer bluster; he sensed Bill's reaction. "Bill, I'm putting it to you straight. Until you learn how to operate as a team member and not just the boss, you're limiting yourself. I need teamwork in my organization just as you need it in yours, and when one man decides he can do everything he makes my job just that much tougher, if not impossible. Let me say it again—and, if you don't hear it this time, I guess you'd better move on somewhere else: You're a great guy and a pillar of strength, but you've got one big fault: You'd rather compete than eat or sleep. Now, the fact is that you aren't a superman—you've got to cooperate with people. You can't drive them all the time, and you can't compete with them all the time. You've got to work with them and *communicate with them as human beings!* When you learn to do that, you'll be ready to move up. I'm sorry it's come to this, but I want you to know how I feel. If a camel is a horse put together by a committee, give me a committee every time. After all, a camel is my idea of a useful animal!"

Bill had not expected to go this far himself, and he was ready to backtrack. "Well, John, I guess both of us sort of let ourselves go. I've certainly got a lot of thinking to do now. And I don't want you to think I was fighting you on this. You're the boss, when all's said and done, and what you say is final."

"No, Bill, what I say is just the beginning. I never get a chance to finish anything around here. The best I can do is to start the right things going and hope that the people working for me will be able to finish them."

This was something Bill had never heard before—the boss admitting that he couldn't accomplish anything on his own. It was a little frightening somehow. Why couldn't the top man do whatever he chose or finish anything he started? "When I'm in John's shoes," Bill thought to himself, "I don't want to have to wait for everybody else to get the job done. I want to be able to do it myself." But what if John was right? What if he *couldn't* do it himself?

"Let's talk about it some more," said John. "Let's have lunch tomorrow."

"O.K., fine." Bill figured this would be a good occasion to get the relationship back on an even keel. But he was no longer on an even keel himself; his whole framework had been wrenched out of shape. For the first time in years, his perspective was out of focus. It would take time to get it fixed.

## Grandstanding and the One-Man Show

Incidents of this sort are more often near misses than the head-on collision this one turned out to be. Nevertheless, they are common in modern-day organizational life. The reason is simple: Most of the rewards of our society and our organizations are geared to recognizing individual performance. Even where a team does pull together effectively, the individual sacrifices his own best interests to the interests of the team and is seldom noticed outside the group itself. He may be highly valued by other team members who know the importance of his contribution, but outsiders see only the stars. Avid football fans may know the names of the linemen on their favorite team, but most of them concentrate on the flashy quarterback, the seatback, or the powerful fullback who is always good for the first-down yardage on the third down.

Movie and recording stars who are individually well known get the fancy contracts at high salaries. Even when team effort is required in the entertainment field, as in popular orchestras or "combos," who knows the name of anyone besides the leader? And, just because he is the man in the organization who is known to the outside world, he usually takes a bigger-than-average share of the pot for himself.

In business, too, we may deplore the grandstander, but we make a star of him and give him the big rewards. The men who move up in large organizations often take with them a trusted staff of subordinates. Indeed, one of the principal assets of many a rising manager is a well-seasoned staff which he has carefully put together along the way and which has developed a precisely tuned system of communication. In many cases, his success depends entirely on his staff, yet outsiders focus their attention on the great man himself; they seldom even realize that a staff goes with him. Should conditions change and his staff no longer work together as well as they did, the leader may become incompetent. But, even if that happens, few people will recognize that his effectiveness has been a group effort rather than a one-man show.

In view of all this, how can we blame Bill Williams for playing the game like a grandstander? How can we fault him on having set out to be the greatest one-man show in the company, capable of meeting every challenge that presents itself? He was only doing "what came naturally." And in fact he has been lucky. At some point every manager discovers that the one-man show is a myth—and sometimes it happens under much more unpleasant circumstances. Having felt himself indispensable in his role as boss, he may fall ill, have to leave for an extended period, and depend on his staff to carry his weight. When he returns, he learns that the job has been done as well as it would have been done if he had been there.

After the initial shock, he settles in. His subordinates bring him problems which came up during his absence and which they were able to solve only tentatively or partially. He begins to see his own role in perspective. He realizes that he is far less important than he once thought he was in terms of actual production; that his major contribution lies in developing competent subordinate managers, helping them to solve problems they cannot cope with alone, and coordinating team effort.

In such a way does the top man develop a new appreciation of teamwork, committees, and the kind of communication they involve. It is a salutary experience—and not at all rare—for a top manager to exceed his abilities and energies only to discover that he still can't get the job done; and the learning is even faster if, when he reaches the limits of his ability, he also courts personal failure. The sudden knowledge that he has, indeed, been playing bet-your-career is like a physical blow.

## The Truly Indispensable Man

The thousands of Bills in the business world who are great performers but are too competitive for sound teamwork with their peers would be wise to consider this fact: It would be foolhardy for a president of General Motors to try to handle all the details involved in producing just one automobile. A man in such a position is not able personally to turn out a single item sold by the organization, yet he plays a singularly valuable role in coordinating the effort of subordinate managers and setting the stage for teamwork throughout the organization.

For there is one exception to the observation made earlier that all the rewards go to the grandstander or the star. That exception is *the well-seasoned modern industrial manager*. His name is not a household word. His identity is probably known only to employees and a few stockholders. If he is a middle manager, he may be familiar to only a small segment of the total organization, yet his contribution may be critical to its success. He is the man who makes teamwork possible in complex organizations dealing with complex technology. Why? Because he is an effective communicator in committees or groups of any sort.

The point has been effectively made by John Kenneth Galbraith in *The New Industrial State*. In this day of modern technology, he declares, few products can be produced singlehandedly. The day when the vice president or general manager of the firm personally knew every detail of its operations is rapidly coming to an end. The only operations he is still likely to know well are those which have not changed in the past 30 years and are probably on the brink of technological obsolescence.

Many products must now be created through the joint efforts of a team of specialists, each contributing his expertise to successful design, production, and marketing. In such a process, effective communication is vital. No one can dominate all the technological aspects of that process without warping the end product out of recognizable shape. Teamwork and team communication are not merely nice ideas for modern organizations; they are absolute necessities.

## Risk Taking and the Group

Bill Williams' complaints about committees are not without foundation. Many groups, teams, and task forces work together in total disharmony and utter incompetence. The opportunities they afford for backstabbing, undermining, politicking, obstructing, and domineering are legion. There are powerful forces operating against their effectiveness: competitiveness, self-confidence, egotism, vanity, greed, jealousy—all centering in the drive for personal status.

There are, nevertheless, some real advantages to committees. In addition to the fact that many modern products could not be manufactured without effective committee-style cooperation, there is the recently discovered phenomenon that, in the process of openly discussing the options and risks inherent in any decision, a well-functioning group tends to accept a larger measure of risk than any one individual in the group would take. Therefore, when the risks that must be taken for the good of the organization are too large for a single manager to tolerate, a committee of some sort may be required before the proper action can be determined.

A pertinent analogy is provided by the original Lloyds of London insurance exchange. Although no single individual was able to insure an entire ship and its cargo, the risk could be shared by having several hundred people assume a fraction of the total burden should the ship be damaged or sunk. Each could easily bear his portion of the possible loss. No one assumed all the risk; but, by the same token, no one individual collected the entire insurance premium. Thus, while the men who formed Lloyds of London forwent the opportunity to rise to the top of the financial community, each had the chance to make an excellent living through marine insurance as long as he accepted the fact that he could never go it alone.

So it is in business and industry today. Groups are essential in the management of a company if the optimum risk is to be assumed and if full advantage is to be taken of modern technology.

## Communication Within Committees

Organizations are set up to motivate human beings by means of disparate rewards. The fact that the president of the corporation earns many times the salary of the laborer on the plant floor is an effective motivator of performance. However, the status, economic privilege, and general awe accorded the president emphasize to the employees, *not* teamwork and effective cooperation, but individual excellence.

The net result is that too many people perceive the job of managing in terms of personal prestige rather than in terms of making a contribution to the workings of the organization. They struggle and claw to achieve status for themselves. Put a number of individuals into a group whose structure is ambiguous, for whom no leader has been appointed, and whose purpose is undefined, and with rare exceptions there will be conflict. This is no idle hypothesis; as was pointed out earlier, it happens often in laboratory training, whose popularity in business today stems from the fact that it addresses itself to the critical need to function and communicate effectively as a member of a group when the status of all members is equal.

When a committee is put together in an organization, it is usually deemed ungentlemanly to get angry or to create open and direct conflict about the issues being considered. The usual unwritten rule is that conflict must not be allowed to erupt; it must be repressed at all costs, lest it reflect on the entire group. Apathy and noninvolvement often prevail. As a result, many committees—ad hoc and otherwise—fail to accomplish what they are set up to do. They fail because they are unable to address themselves to the real problems underlying the one they are supposed to solve. And they cannot address themselves to these underlying problems because to do so would require that they acknowledge the differences in perspective among the members and these differences in perspective cannot be openly aired without risking conflict.

One individual may seize upon an accident of seniority, a seat at the head of the table, or his ability to talk longer or louder than anyone else and thereby dominate the group. By doing so, however, he exposes himself to criticism from the other members of the group, who are likely to point out his ineptness as a leader and to resist his self-conferred authority. If a leader is appointed by the sanctioning organization, much the same thing happens, though somewhat less openly: People with strong competitive instincts who are put into a group where their status is little different from anyone else's may resist direction or domination by either designated or would-be leaders.

Laboratory training gets at these problems rather effectively. In the typical training session, the total lack of structure or assigned status often leads an all-out dogfight for control of the group. Both active and passive styles of operation soon emerge, and individuals with strong competitive tendencies almost immediately find themselves in open conflict. They jockey and maneuver to obtain and hold the advantage. Some people single out other members of the group who appear to be pliable or sympathetic and attempt to form coalitions. If this doesn't work, they may try to persuade the rest of the group to appoint as leader someone whom they are sure they can influence on important issues.

Destructive tactics also may be used. Some people adopt the attitude, "If I don't run the group, nobody will." They try, at all costs, to prevent anyone else from taking over the leadership, even in an informal, unstructured group. Their own desire to command is so strong that they will not yield to anyone.

The tactics that work best in unstructured group activity are openness, cooperation, sensitivity, ability to listen, and responsiveness to the needs of other people. For the would-be leader, the only formula for success is to put himself at the disposal of the group, to serve it in any way it may wish—from general housekeeper to errand boy. Because the other members are generally anxious to have someone available who will do what they want done, anyone who agrees to that role is automatically a hero. He may, of course, be debased in the process; but he may end up closer to being the leader than anyone else, precisely because he is willing and able to serve the group effectively.

## Effective Committee and Conference Leadership

A close look at almost any voluntary group—church, service club, or association—will reveal that the most industrious and conscientious member is usually the president. He is usually recognized as "a sucker for work."

One of the surest ways to achieve status in such an organization is to prove your worthiness by giving unstintingly of your effort and money. The world is full of people who have learned that the easy way out is to let the man who needs the status have it as long as he does the work. Many a president has exhausted himself finding this out, yet there is a good deal of common sense in this kind of logic.

The biggest problem of any group, whether it be an informal association or a formally organized business, is the effective utilization of its resources. People with the necessary energy and ability must somehow be encouraged to use those qualities so as to achieve the objectives of the organization. What better way to do this than through some sort of reward? The principal reward is money, although status, privilege, and recognition are closely correlated with it. And in many voluntary organizations, the only direct reward is status.

All this leads to the question at hand: how to lead a committee, conference, or task force. Although much has been written on the subject, a good deal of it concentrates on the mechanical aspects of the process—adhering to parliamentary procedure, eliciting participation, or—most belabored of all—resolving disputes. Yet these are all secondary; the most important element of such leadership is *hard work on behalf of the group*...

At first glance, this statement may seem idealistic or even moralistic. "Sure," you may say, "any good leader puts his shoulder to the wheel and does his job effectively." It is, however, a very practical and unsentimental principle. No one in a committee of equals is more reviled than a chairman who leaves all the work to everyone else; the leader who fails to work hard for his group risks loss of respect and a badly tarnished reputation. To be effective, then, a group leader must be a very busy fellow. Bill Williams undoubtedly thinks that this means being personally productive, and certainly this is an important factor in leadership. The effective leader is a working leader in every sense of the word. But it is not enough to be productive and set a good example. Because the committee chairman cannot discipline people and hasn't enough rewards and privileges at his disposal for motivating them to be productive, he must somehow influence them through other means.

A good committee chairman therefore needs highly developed skills in many areas. He must

> ✧ Be sensitive to the personal needs of each member as a human being. Be prepared to work out ways to satisfy those needs and so motivate each individual to become an effective contributor. Be able to let genuine differences of opinion come out into the open, even when conflict is the result.
> ✧ Be effective at focusing differences of opinion on the purposes and objectives of the committee, rather than letting the group founder on personalities or mutual recriminations. So that the full resources of the group may be brought into play, see that all differences are fully explored at the beginning.
> ✧ Learn the special capabilities of each group member and harness them to the work of the group as appropriate.
> ✧ Learn to listen in order to understand the processes going on in the group and be fully responsive to them. Never

make the mistake of becoming absorbed in personal concerns and fears.

In short, the effective committee chairman must be willing to do his best for little more than the hollow distinction of being accorded the title and status of leader.

In many quarters, it has long been held that the manager does not work; he delegates. But is this really different from getting the members of a committee to participate actively in its work? There are many similarities between the two situations: the manager with his employees and the group leader with his committee or task force. The good group leader is likely to be a good manager, and vice versa, and the skills needed are the same ones that must be used to obtain more than adequate performance in every organization. To be sure, we can maintain attendance and minimum production by threats of removal from the payroll or other punishment. We may also be able to drive, cajole, persuade, and intimidate people into doing a little more. But we can never obtain wholehearted commitment to the activities of the committee or the work group until we learn to involve people. This, indeed, is the job of managing and the job of committee leadership.

## The Payoff of Committee Communication

Committee, conference, and task-force work in an organizational context need not be mere special-purpose activity and need not be limited to unique situations. Any time a manager has a relatively important problem to solve, he may well delegate it to a group for exploration and recommendations. There are a number of reasons for doing this on a regular basis.

To begin with, committees, conferences, and task forces are effective in breaking down old habits of noncommunication among functions in an organization. Getting people together in unusual groupings forces a certain amount of interaction which increases familiarity and, at the very least, opens the door to developing an understanding of one another's problems. It engenders the informal, cross-functional lines of communication which, though ignored on the organizational chart, are vital to organizational success.

Then, too, performance in special-purpose groups is an excellent way to let people with growth and promotion potential be seen by a wide range of managers other than their immediate superiors. In other words, they can demonstrate their abilities to people who do not ordinarily see them in action. Executives higher in the organization can judge these individuals for themselves, thereby supplementing the evaluations of those for whom they normally work and counteracting any biases and prejudices that may exist. Also, as a further developmental fringe benefit, people who would like to change their field of specialization or take on cross-functional assignments are in a position to become sufficiently well known that managers of other departments will be inclined to consider them. The individual whose capabilities are known only through the reports of his immediate manager is too often overlooked; committees and task forces make it possible to recognize and develop him so that he may be put to more constructive use.

Working on a committee, conference, or task force permits the individual to perform in a new frame of reference. The exposure may well lead to increased stimulation and interest in his overall job. More to the point, both the man who is regarded as a standout by his superior and the man whose potential is unknown because he is submerged in his work group can be tested in the new setting to see if their performance is consistent or is merely a result of special job conditions. Such testing is eminently useful, inasmuch as reputation alone is not a reliable basis for judgment; a good many stars are actually standing on other people's shoulders, and not a few quiet plodders carry a much heavier load than anyone gives them credit for.

Finally, the man who can get results through other people without having formal control over their pay checks is indeed an effective all-around leader and communicator. He has had excellent preparation for managerial duties.

### The Toughest Kind of Leadership

We can understand why a man like Bill Williams objects to committees. To be effective as a member, he must put aside his competitive instincts. He cannot be a one-man show—or, if he is, he must be prepared to do *all* the work. Leadership in the context of the special team is the toughest kind to achieve. There are no easy ways to force people into line and make them productive. Anyone who believes in the power of authority is bound to be both dismayed and distressed at finding himself so helpless.

In addition, a highly competitive manager like Bill is likely to use every tool at his disposal to gain and keep the upper hand—including the tool of withholding information. Having his subordinates assigned to task forces generally means dilution of the rigid control of communication which he may be accustomed to maintaining; as a result of committee activities, he may be faced with a freer flow of information and greater openness of communication within the organization. And, if he senses that possibility, he will not be eager to have *his* evaluation of his employees cross-checked against the evaluations of other managers. In extreme cases, the competitive manager closes his group up tight and permits information out of it or into it only through himself. Team effort is clearly repugnant to him.

Perhaps we can understand the dilemma of manager John Wilson, too. In order to get Bill to see the need for a change in his style of operating, it will probably be necessary for John to order Bill to use committees. That is the only way in which Bill will ever understand their utility; as long as he is allowed to avoid them, he will continue to condemn them wholesale. Certainly, as higher management becomes more aware of the importance of broadening the lines of communication within the organization rather than restricting them, and as it recognizes the advantages of committees, conferences, and task forces as information and communication tools, pressure to increase their use will undoubtedly magnify. John will then have to see that Bill makes his peace with committees. His acquiescence may not be altogether graceful, but acquiescence there will have to be. The reason is simple: Bill runs a one-man show, and no one-man show can equal a good organization with good internal lines of communication. Every organization needs the open, easy flow of communication between its components that teams engender.

In the final analysis, Bill will have to develop full communication effectiveness. If he understands the impact of committees on organizational communication and, thus, on organizational effectiveness, he may be better able to make his adjustment.

# 12

------ ◆ ------

## Conclusions

HARVEY HANCOCK was on his feet again. "I still say it all boils down to communication!" he said. His tone was a little less pompous and overbearing than before, but his aggressive self-confidence was still there. "We've talked about all kinds of communication, but the nub of the matter is this: When we communicate with employees, we just want to get through. Don't we?" This time he didn't try to answer his own question.

A quiet voice spoke up: "It's pretty hard to argue with the idea that everything boils down to communication, but it seems to me that the statement glosses over more than it explains. What disturbs me is that there used to be some limit to what could and should be communicated in a business setting. Nowadays it seems as though the boss is always trying to get you to spill your guts and convince you to do the same thing with your staff."

Sounds of agreement were heard around the room.

"I agree," someone chimed in. "My boss told me I didn't know how to listen and sent me off to one of those 'sensitivity training' deals. I've never been through so much hell in one week in all my life. They badgered me, shouted at me, and belittled me until I felt like an idiot. I don't think anybody has the right to make anybody else talk about his own affairs. I'd as soon stick to the ritualized communication we've been talking about."

"I've tried opening up to employees and establishing close personal contact with them," added a youngish man, "and it's dynamite. You should never get on a personal plane with the people you work with. I almost lost my job because my secretary thought I was trying to make her when all I was doing was being a little informal in my communication."

"Have you ever tried leveling with your boss and telling him what you really feel?" still another voice asked the room in general. "I did that once, and I'll never do it again. He treated me like an escapee from a psycho ward from then on."

The instructor took the floor again. "I think what we're expressing here is the fact that most people do *not* communicate openly, fully, and intimately except in very special circumstances. Most of our day-to-day communication is highly conventional and formal. We deal with one another at arm's length and exchange only stylized messages. The truth of the matter is that much of the time we don't *want* to know what other people are really thinking and feeling."

## Communication in a Business Setting

"Just last week," continued the instructor, "I had an experience of this sort in a small restaurant near my office. I dropped in for lunch a little late, and the crowd was beginning to thin out. My waitress was obviously harassed, and as I sat down she spilled a cup of coffee on her hand. She was a very pretty girl, but the language she used was enough to make a sailor blush. I blushed myself, in fact. When I thought about it though, I realized it wasn't the language that made me uncomfortable, it was the fact that this girl was openly expressing her feelings in my presence. She was cursing her fate in my hearing. She almost immediately realized my embarrassment and began telling me what had gone wrong in the restaurant that day. Her explanation only made matters worse. I had gone there for a quiet, relaxed lunch only to find myself hip-deep in someone else's troubles, and at that moment I didn't really want any part of them. I guess the rule of thumb to follow is this: If you want someone to commiserate with you, find someone who is already as miserable as you are."

Harvey Hancock's eyes lit up; he had the opening he wanted. "Who said that if you want to communicate with someone you have to get down on all fours and crawl? Business communication should always be businesslike."

"On the contrary," said the instructor, "communication in a business setting should be effective in terms of business objectives. You should choose the technique that serves the needs of the company and your own needs as well. Formal communication—the businesslike kind you've been talking about—serves most of these needs. But the needs it doesn't serve are the ones that can destroy a career or even a business."

"You don't understand!" Harvey blurted out, but nobody was listening to him. It was clear now that he could communicate in only one way, that he had nothing further to contribute to this seminar.

Fortunately for the Harvey Hancocks of this world, most business communication is designed to insure that in its simplest form— the formal one-way message—it will be heeded and acted upon by the employees to whom it is addressed. Too often, however, communication never gets beyond the one-way channeling of instructions or information. When problems of individual feeling and preferences arise, there is no mechanism for dealing with them.

Indeed, one of the great drawbacks in business communication is that personal feelings and preferences are often ruled out as not proper forms. Whenever anyone gets emotional, someone chides, "Let's leave personal feelings out of this."

## Rationality and Its Limitations

The implication of such admonitions is that all business communication should be rational; and, certainly, rationality is a powerful force in dealing with business problems. Unfortunately, however, rationality is useful in solving only *simple* problems. Complex decisions—who should be president of the company, what product should be dropped or developed for next year's marketing effort, how to insure high productivity while at the same time giving bright young managerial talent wide exposure to a variety of operations—do not yield readily to cold, logical treatment. Whenever we must deal with value preferences, we must somehow develop the capacity to cope with our own feelings and those of others.

Too often, so-called logical decision making is nothing but an argumentative exercise through which personal preference, bias, or feeling is expressed symbolically. The result is a considerable loss of energy and little or no rational communication. Too many managers reach an impasse because they have failed to confront one another with the real issues. When communication within the business setting is restricted to logical, rational, and unemotional issues, the resulting intensity of the need to express personal preferences and desires may eventually make it impossible to communicate at all.

Our culture has traditionally constrained men in general, and businessmen in particular, from displays of emotion on the grounds that they are signs of weakness. Candid, informal communication is customarily restricted to fraternity brothers and drinking cronies. Many organizations would be unable to function were it not for some local lodge or service group which sanctions and encourages informal, personal exchange among its members.

In part, too, the problem stems from a lack of skill in articulating feelings. Men, especially businessmen, find so few opportunities to practice emotional communicative techniques that they may never learn to open up with other people.

## The "Bridge" Analogy

The highly popular game of bridge probably exemplifies the present state of communication in our society better than any other activity we could cite.

In bridge, one player must communicate his holdings to his partner in a formal and stylized fashion. Informal communication is forbidden and may be penalized, especially in supervised tournaments. A good bridge player develops a high degree of skill in communicating his holdings and preferences with limited cues, and novices soon discover that they can make themselves understood much better with some partners than with others.

The most effective communication is between partners who use the same relative degree of complexity in their bids (cues) and who have played together long enough to know each other's style. Bidding in bridge (that is, communicating) follows a set of explicit rules and should be entirely rational. However, the range of situations people face even in a bridge game is such that a certain amount of flexibility in bidding is necessary to communicate one's holdings, and certain illogical (that is, emotional) styles develop with avid players and regular partners.

Communication in real life conforms to the bridge pattern to a considerable degree. It follows a set of rules, some implicit and some explicit, which insure that the essential messages are conveyed while at the same time permitting a small amount of individual style. Such tactics severely limit the number of symbols which can be used, and a vast number of symbols remain unused.

To insure that essential messages get across, we limit the range of conventional communicative cues we use every day. This leaves us with two worlds of communication: the formal world of conventional communication and the informal world of private, personal communication. Because our most personal messages can be understood only by people who know us well, and because so few people do know us to any extent, we carefully restrict ourselves to those who have demonstrated trust, understanding, and empathy toward us in the past. Close friends with whom we can communicate on a personal level are added to our select circle only through a special process. They must be vouched for by a trusted friend, or they must prove themselves trustworthy in circumstances that leave us no choice except to be open and candid.

## Opening the Channels

Clearly, communication is most efficient when we are candid and open. If, in a bridge game, we were to ignore the rules and speak informally with our partner until each of us was satisfied with his estimate of the other's holdings, we could probably be much more effective in determining our prospects for winning. If, in the business setting, we could expose and express our personal needs and preferences directly without fear, and if we could accept openness as a regular pattern, the average organization would operate more efficiently, more effectively, and more profitably. This is because the best energies of the participants would no longer be focused on dealing with one another and could be concentrated on dealing with the market place.

Perhaps such a degree of openness is a hopelessly idealistic goal. Businesses are structured so that their members (employees and managers) are in competition for the available monetary, status, and other rewards. This competition is incompatible with candor. Communication is conventional and "businesslike" simply because this is the safest kind to use in a competitive setting. As a result, any small group of people who can communicate without fear or distrust of one another can very nearly take over the organization and run it.

The recriminations we so often hear about "playing politics" are really only indications that such cliques do develop, whether by accident or by design, and that communication within them is so much more effective than the usual, formal type that the members have a distinct advantage over everyone else. But the aims and objectives of such groups are not always in the best interests of the organization. Effective informal communication aimed at the achievement of objectives that are not business oriented can create a very real problem.

## Conventional Techniques No Longer Sufficient

In many organizations today, formal, conventional communication is no longer sufficient. A wide range of techniques must now be employed in order to build and maintain an effective organization. The businessman who does not recognize his need to develop a broad spectrum of communicative skills is limiting his ability to deal with today's problems.

Certain it is that many problems will arise as business communication makes the transition from formal channels to an increasing number of informal, open channels. Laboratory training for business managers is already in the throes of a substantial controversy centering around the invasion of privacy and the right to privacy. Many people believe that emotional communication in a business setting is innately wrong. But businessmen who are to solve their problems will have to use the skills of informal communication—even if only selectively.

It will always be necessary to preserve the right to remain personally uninvolved and the right to avoid embarrassment. The fact is, however, that skill in direct personal communication is becoming more and more necessary if one is to succeed as a manager. The lack of such skill can be detrimental to one's career and to the effectiveness of one's business as well.

Communication has been compared to bidding a hand at bridge, but it is far more than that. It is a richly varied and complex process which offers numerous possibilities for exchanging ideas and information. It has profiles yet to be perceived. The new face of communication has yet to be fully seen; the potential rewards are unlimited if communication is used wisely and well.

# INDEX

# Index

199

# About the Author

GLENN A. BASSETT is Consultant, Personnel Systems at General Electric Company corporate headquarters. He holds degrees from the University of California and California State College, and he has done advanced study at the University of Southern California.

Mr. Bassett was field representative for Travelers Insurance Company and acting manager of employment and industrial psychologist for Climax Molybdenum Company before joining General Electric Company in 1962. Prior to his present post he served as manager, relations program development and evaluation, for General Electric's Apollo Support Department in Daytona Beach, Florida.

Mr. Bassett is the author of two books, *Practical Interviewing* (1965) and *Management Styles in Transition* (1966), and a recording, *Communicating Both Ways*. All were published by the American Management Association.